WordStar®

Made Easy

Second Edition

Walter A. Ettlin

Osborne/McGraw-Hill
Berkeley, California

Published by
Osborne/McGraw-Hill
630 Bancroft Way
Berkeley, California   94710
U.S.A.

For information on translations and book distributors outside
of the U.S.A., please write Osborne/McGraw-Hill at the
above address.

WORDSTAR® MADE EASY, Second Edition

  2 3 4 5 6 7 8 9 0 GBGB 89876543

ISBN 0-931988-90-X

Cover design by Yashi Okita.

Text design by KLT van Genderen.

Acknowledgments

I would like to thank the following people:

Lee Parr, my secretary, who suffered through the early learning stages of WordStar with me and did most of the initial editing of this manual.

Brenda Aguilar, a high school student, who "translated" my initial handwritten version of this manual to WordStar.

Cynthia, my wife, who was pressed into duty at various stages, usually on a moment's notice, to edit, translate, or just listen to ideas.

Mary Borchers, Editorial Director of Osborne/McGraw-Hill, who offered many suggestions, helped with the final editing, and coordinated all the tasks necessary to bring this manual to completion.

W.A.E.

Contents

Introduction

The purpose of this manual is to help you become proficient with WordStar. WordStar is a very flexible word processing program published by MicroPro International Corporation. This manual will give you the skill required for most types of general word processing assignments. The skills you acquire in completing the exercises in this manual can be applied to word processors in any type of business office.

This book is not intended to replace the *WordStar User's Guide* published by MicroPro. The MicroPro manual will supplement the command descriptions presented here, as well as introduce any WordStar commands not covered in this book. For each instruction discussed, we indicate the section in the MicroPro manual where the same instruction is covered. Depending on which version of WordStar you are using, the section reference will be indicated within the following characters:

< >   Version 1.x

{ }   Version 2.x if different than Version 1.x. (If no braces are shown, refer to the section for Version 1.x)

[ ]   Version 3.x. (Refers to page, rather than section, number)

1

Each lesson contains a set of instructions, sample exercises, and example text to be used in the lesson. If you have followed all the instructions, the text displayed on your screen or printed on your printer should match the example text in this book.

Second Edition

The main additions to WordStar 3.0 are new and better organized menus, side scrolling (to make it easier to work with long lines), and the ability to block off and move columns. In addition to covering the powerful new features of Micropro's WordStar 3.0, this second edition also covers MailMerge and SpellStar.

MailMerge and SpellStar are programs purchased separately from WordStar, but you must have WordStar in order to use them. MailMerge allows you to create form letters with text automatically inserted from data files or from the keyboard; it also has many other features. SpellStar has two main features: first, to compare words in your file against a 20,000-word dictionary that is supplied, and second, to maintain or create new dictionaries. Even though these are separate programs, we assume you are familiar with WordStar before you attempt the lessons dealing with these two programs.

Instructions for the
WordStar Command Sheet

You will use the *WordStar Command Sheet,* located at the back of this book, while working with WordStar, so have it handy any time you are at the computer. The command sheet is a summary of the most commonly used commands in the WordStar manual. You might want to remove it from this book and keep it near your computer for quick reference. The sooner you fully understand the commands listed on the sheet, the better you will be at using WordStar.

The symbol ^ stands for the CTRL (Control) key, which is located on the left-hand side of the computer keyboard. The CTRL key on a computer is always used in conjunction with another key. Like a shift key, the CTRL key must be held down while the other key is pressed.

Unlike the shift key, though, the code sent by the CTRL key does not register on the screen. It commands WordStar to perform some editing or formatting function, such as setting margins, underlining, or saving a document on the disk. You will use the CTRL key a great deal when working with WordStar.

The arrows at the upper left of the command sheet indicate the direction the cursor will move when the CTRL key and the indicated letter are pressed together. The *cursor* is the line or box on the computer screen that indicates where your next keystroke will appear. You will use all of these features as you learn to use WordStar.

Getting Started

When you are working with WordStar you are actually working with two computer programs: WordStar and CP/M. *CP/M* (Control Program Monitor) is the disk operating system; it performs its functions automatically. See the Appendix for more information on CP/M.

Load WordStar

Turn on the computer. Your system will have from one to four disk drives. Place your WordStar disk in drive A and close the door. Because of the various manufacturers supporting WordStar, you will have to refer to your user's guide for proper start-up procedures. Simply closing the door on drive A is sufficient for start-up on some systems. The disk drive will start, and in a few seconds you will get the CP/M sign-on message, something like the following:

```
CP/M VER.2.2

A>
```

The message will vary according to your system or source of CP/M, but the A> prompt is standard. The letter A tells you that you are operating from disk drive A. The greater-than symbol (>) is the prompt for CP/M and tells you the program is ready to accept a command. You must always start the computer with a disk containing CP/M in drive A.

To load WordStar, type **WS** (characters you are to type in are indicated in boldface type) and press RETURN.

```
CP/M VER.2.2

A>WS ←—— Press RETURN
```

WordStar Menu

When WordStar is loaded you will be presented with a main WordStar menu. A program *menu* lets you select one item from a list of options. This menu is called the "no-file" menu, because you are not yet working with a specific text file.

```
                      <<<NO-FILE MENU>>>

* * * Preliminary Commands * * * | * File Commands * | *System Commands *
  L   Change logged disk drive   |                   | R Run a program
  F   File directory     off (ON) | P  Print a file  | X Exit to system
  H   Set help level             |                   |
  *  * Commands to Open a File *  *| E Rename a file  |* WordStar Operations*
  D   Open a document file        | O Copy a a file   | M Run MailMerge
  N   Open a non-document file    | Y Delete a file   | S Run SpellStar


DIRECTORY of disk A:
```

Let's go through this Version 3.x menu and try some of the options now. Version 1.x and 2.x menus will not include all of the options shown here.

Preliminary Commands (L, F, H)

[1-3]   **L** — Change logged disk drive. Press **L** and you will be asked the disk drive to change to. If you have more than one disk drive, you can keep WordStar data files separate from the actual program file. To work on data files in drive B, you would enter **B:** and then press RETURN. You must type the colon after the drive identifier. The screen will change to indicate that you are logged to drive B and display the names of files that are on the disk in drive B (called the *directory*).

If you have two disk drives, it's a good idea to use your second drive for text files, with WordStar itself in the first drive. After loading WordStar change your logged disk drive for your text files before you begin working with those files.

F — File directory off (ON). Press **F** and notice that the no-file menu indicates the file directory is off and the directory is no longer on the screen. Press **F** again and the directory reappears.

H — Set help levels. Press **H** and you are presented with a new menu of "help levels." You may choose from the options given. When you begin working on a word processing file, you will see that the amount of work displayed on the screen is affected by how much "help" is also displayed. Working with the level set to 2 or less suppresses the menus and allows more room on the screen for your text. (This value can be set permanently at whatever level you wish with the WordStar install program.)

Commands to Open a File (D, N)

D — Open a document file. Normally when you work with WordStar, you will press **D** for a document file. Don't press **D** just yet, but wait until we are ready to start Lesson 1.

N — Open a non-document file. The N option, for non-document file, is used when you want to create a data file for use with MailMerge or when you wish to write or edit a program for BASIC.

File Commands (P, E, O, Y)

These commands require a text file in order to perform their function. Since you are just starting and do not have a file to work with, we will not illustrate these now. These commands are presented in Lesson 3.

System Commands (R, X)

R — Run a program. Pressing **R** allows you to run programs with file extension COM, found on most of the utility programs in CP/M. The most common use is to run STAT.COM to check space available on your disk. An overview of STAT is given in the CP/M appendix.

X — Exit to system. Pressing **X** returns you to the CP/M system management program, which is where you were before you loaded the WordStar program.

WordStar Operations (M, S)

M — MailMerge. This option is covered in Lessons 15, 16, and 17.

S — SpellStar. This option is presented in Lesson 18.

Start a Text File

To begin word processing you'll use a *text,* or "document," file. Whether you're entering text for the first time or correcting text, this process is referred to as *editing* a file.

To edit a file, first type **D** from the WordStar no-file menu. You will be asked the name of the file. Type in **EXAMPLE.1** (in naming a file you may use up to eight letters or numbers, then a period, and a combination of up to three letters or numbers as an *extension* after the period; the extension is optional). Remember that you should be logged into your text file drive before starting your document file (use L from the WordStar no-file menu).

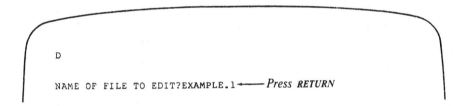

```
D


NAME OF FILE TO EDIT?EXAMPLE.1 ◄── Press RETURN
```

The data on the screen has now changed again and should show the main menu. Now type ^**JH** (whenever you see the symbol ^, press the CTRL key and hold it down while pressing the letter immediately following the symbol ^). A new menu, entitled Help Levels, will appear on the screen (see Lesson 14 for menu samples). Type **0** and the screen will show two important lines:

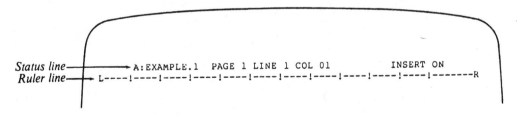

```
Status line──────► A:EXAMPLE.1  PAGE 1 LINE 1 COL 01          INSERT ON
Ruler line────► L----!----!----!----!----!----!----!----!----!----!----!-------R
```

At the very top is the *status line,* which tells you the name of the file you are working on, the page number, and the line number and column number where the cursor is located. The second line is the *ruler line,* which will be explained in future lessons.

Notice the series of dots that appear down the right side of the screen. The dot is one of a variety of *flag characters*. Flag characters always appear in column 80 on the screen. Flag characters are non-printing characters that indicate a variety of different types of lines that are entered on the screen. They will be discussed in later lessons.

Now on to Lesson 1.

Cursor Movement
Scrolling

In the Getting Started section, you should have prepared to start a text file or word processing document named EXAMPLE.1. Now, using text in Example 1 at the end of this chapter, just start typing. Don't worry about typing errors now. You need not press RETURN when you near the end of a line as you would do on a typewriter. As you type, press RETURN *only at the end of each paragraph.* Due to WordStar's *word wrap* feature, which is on by default, text that would extend past the right margin is automatically "wrapped around" to the left margin of the next line.

Watch the screen as you come to the end of a line and notice how the last letters of the last word on each line are lined up in the same column. This is called *right justification.* Text is right-justified by default. Extra spaces are inserted between words so that the last character of each line ends up at the right margin. To skip a line between paragraphs, simply press RETURN again. Don't worry about any mistakes; we'll take care of those in a later lesson.

Notice the *flag* character (<) in column 80. This symbol indicates that RETURN was pressed on that line. This flag character identifies, or "flags," the end of any paragraph.

Cursor Movement (^Q, ^S, ^E, ^D, ^X)

<8.01>
[3-1]
Refer to the command sheet and use the CTRL key and the letter next to the arrow to move the cursor in the direction indicated by the arrow. ^E moves the cursor up one line, ^S moves the cursor one space to the left, ^D moves the cursor one space to the right, and ^X moves the cursor one line down. Notice what happens when the cursor is at the extreme right of a line and ^D is pressed once more: the cursor will move to the left end of the line below. On the last line of a paragraph when ^X is pressed, the cursor will move to the left-hand side of the next line on the screen.

Notice that the letters S, E, D, and X on the keyboard form a diamond shape. The cursor moves in the direction represented by the positions of these keys.

Press ^Q and the letter E. The cursor will now be at the top of the screen. Combining ^Q with the cursor movement keys enables you to move the cursor quickly to the top, bottom, left, or right side of the screen. Keep in mind the shape of this cluster of keys.

```
                         Top
                         ^QE
                          △
          Left ^QS  ◁          ▷   ^QD Right
                          ▽
                         ^QX
                       Bottom
```

Right Word, Left Word (^F, ^A)

<8.01>
[3-1]
Now place the cursor at the top left-hand side of the screen. Press ^F four or five times and notice how the cursor moves quickly to the first letter of the word to the right. Place the cursor at the right end of any line, and press ^A several times. Notice how this moves the cursor to the first letter of the word to the left.

Scrolling (^Z, ^R, ^W, ^C)

<8.02>   *Scrolling* may be a new term to you, so we will define it before going on.
[3-5]   Think of material you have entered into the computer as being on one
long sheet of paper — a scroll. And think of the screen as an opening or
window through which you can see only a small section of that long
sheet of paper. When the window moves up that long sheet of paper and
you see the material you have first written, you are scrolling up, and
when the window moves down the sheet toward the end of the text, you
are scrolling down.

The scrolling commands are very useful when you are reading a
document on the screen. There are four of these commands: ^Z —
scroll down line, ^R — scroll down screen, ^W — scroll up line, and
^C — scroll up screen. To many people the references to up and down
seem backward, but if you think of the screen as a window moving up or
down over the material you typed in, then it makes sense.

Version 3.x users will discover in Lesson 13 that WordStar will scroll
the screen left and right, as well.

End of Lesson 1

When you have finished working with Example 1, press ^K and then the
letter X. The material you have just typed in will be saved on the disk in
the logged drive of the computer. (Saving material will be discussed
further in Lesson 3.) When you use this material for Lesson 2, you'll
just read it into the computer from the disk without retyping. That's one
of the advantages of word processing.

EXERCISES

1. Using Example 1, practice scrolling and moving the cursor to a predetermined position with as few keystrokes as possible.

EXAMPLE 1   15

Most applications of microprocessing in our schools have been on a very small scale and, it seems to me, that what we need at the moment is demonstration of specific benefits which might be realized from the purchase and installation of microcomputers. We currently have thirteen Apple II Plus computers at our school and an Apple III on order; but our program is an exception to the norm in public secondary education.

Our conference theme, therefore, will focus on the use of microcomputers in the public secondary school setting and will incorporate presentations designed to increase awareness in our administration as to the potential benefits of having microcomputers in their schools. I would envision presentations being made in computer assisted science curriculum materials, as multi-discipline tools, and administrative applications of microcomputers.

Margins
Reform Paragraph
Spacing

Load WordStar, and when the menu appears, change your logged disk drive if needed, and press **D** to edit a document file. This means you've already entered and saved a document, and now want to go back and make changes to it, or want to begin another file. A question will appear asking the name of the file you wish to edit. You want to edit the previous file. The name of the file typed in Lesson 1 is EXAMPLE.1, so type in **EXAMPLE.1** and press RETURN. Now appearing on the screen is the material you previously typed, including any mistakes you may have made.

Depending on how your WordStar program was installed, the status line may say INSERT ON. If it does, type ^V to remove this condition. The insert command will be discussed in Lesson 5.

```
       A:EXAMPLE.1   PAGE 1 LINE 1 COL 01        INSERT ON
  L----!----!----!----!----!----!----!----!----!----!----!------R
      '    '    '    '    '    '    '    '    '    '  '   '   '
      '    '    '    '    '    '    '    '    '    '  '   '   '
      '    '    '    '    '    '    '    '    '    '  '   '   '
```

Margins (^OL, ^OR)

<7.3>   The line at the top of the screen is called the ruler line. Notice that the
[2-12]   left and right margins of the material you typed in correspond with the
          left and right ends of the ruler line. You change margins by adjusting the
          length of the ruler line. Other features of the ruler line will be discussed
          in Lesson 4.

<8.06>   We will now change the length of the ruler line. Strike the keys ^O
[4-2]   and L (the ^O keys must be pressed first). There is now a question at
          the top of the screen asking where you want to set the left margin.
          Indicate your choice (a number between 5 and 10, for example) and
          press RETURN. The number you choose determines the column number
          where the material you type in will begin. Notice that the ruler line has
          adapted to begin at the column you indicated. Now, in a similar manner,
          set the right-hand margin. Press ^O and R. In response to the question,
          enter a number between 50 and 65, and press RETURN; again notice how
          the ruler line adapts.

              Now place the cursor directly under the left-hand edge of the ruler
          line and type a single character. Using ^S, move the cursor back over
          the character. Check that the column number indicated in the status line
          is the same as the response you gave when you set the left-hand margin.
          Move the cursor under the right-hand edge of the ruler line by pressing
          the space bar until it has reached the proper position, and see if your
          response to setting the right-hand margin is confirmed by the column
          number indicated in the status line.

Hyphen Help ON/OFF (^OH)

[4-11]   It is sometimes desirable to hyphenate long words at the end of a line,
          and sometimes not. Usually you will hyphenate if you are using a ruler

line of 50 columns or less. When you open a document file hyphen help is ON (see Chapter 14 for menu sample). This option makes it possible for you to automatically hyphenate words. Type ^O and **H** to turn hyphen help OFF. Press ^O and **H** again to turn hyphen help ON. This hyphen help functions only when you reform paragraphs. So, on to the next section.

Reform Paragraph (^B)

<8.06>   First we will reform a paragraph with hyphen help OFF.

[4-2]   Move the cursor to the first letter on the first line of the material you have typed. Press ^**B**. This adjusts, or reforms, all of the text in the first paragraph to fit within the margins determined by the new ruler line.

The cursor is now at the beginning of the second paragraph. By pressing ^**B** again, this paragraph is also reformed. This process can be repeated to reform all the material in any document, regardless of length.

Go back to the beginning of the first paragraph. Press ^O and **H** again to put hyphen help ON. Reform the paragraph again by pressing ^**B**. When the cursor stops on a long word, you have the option of pressing - (a hyphen) to insert a hyphen at the position of the cursor, moving the cursor right or left before pressing -, or pressing ^**B** to continue reforming the paragraph without any hyphen.

^**B** starts the paragraph reform wherever the cursor is positioned at the time, and will reform text until it reaches a RETURN flag (usually at the end of a paragraph) or a hyphen option. If you find that you have an unwanted RETURN character at the end of a line in the middle of a paragraph, here is one way to delete that RETURN: Put the cursor on the first character of the line *after* the RETURN character. Delete characters (DEL key or ^**G**, discussed in Lesson 5) until the line jumps up to the end of the previous line. Then press ^**B** to reform the paragraph.

Line Spacing (^OS)

<8.06>   With WordStar you can set the spacing for the material you are typing to

[4-6]   anything from single space, as it was for Example 1, to one line every nine spaces. You can also easily change the spacing for material that is

already in the computer. Let's try this now. Type ^**OS**. You are asked to choose a value from 1 to 9. To double space, type **2**.

```
^OS     A:EXAMPLE.1   PAGE 1 LINE 1 COL 01
ENTER space OR NEW LINE SPACING (1-9):2 ◄──── Press RETURN

L----!----!----!----!----!----!----!----!----!----!----!-----R
    '   '   '   '   '   '   '   '   '   '   '   '
  '  '    '  '     '   '   '
    '  '    '  '
```

If you do not enter in a new number (that is, if you simply press RETURN), WordStar will enter the *default value.* Default value refers to the automatic values that WordStar uses unless you change them. In the case of spacing, the default value is 1, or single space. Any default value may be changed with the appropriate command to suit the file you are working in. Now move the cursor to the beginning of the first paragraph and reform the paragraph (^**B**). You can repeat the ^**B** command until you have double spaced the entire document.

1. Type in Example 2. Set the left margin to 5 and the right to 40. Reform the paragraphs to fit the margins.

2. Set the left margin to 1 and the right to 78. Reform the paragraphs to fit the margins.

3. Set the margins to whatever you like. Reform the paragraphs to fit the margins.

4. What would happen if you entered a number for the left margin that was larger than the number entered for the right margin? Try it.

EXAMPLE 2

Computer Assisted Instruction (CAI)

An example of this type of program is the Milliken Math sequence. It consists of a comprehensive mathematics curriculum for grades one through six. The advantage being that instruction is completely individualized based on each student's needs and abilities.

The programs are success oriented and provide structured drill with immediate feedback and reinforcement. Students work at their own pace toward mastering specific skills. The time-consuming chores of grading and record keeping are done automatically, providing the teacher with more time for other instructional activities. Perhaps the greatest benefit is the motivational power of the computer.

Saving
Printing
Other File Commands

LESSON 3

In this lesson we'll continue to work with Example 1 text. Load the text file just as you did in Lesson 2. Or, if you don't need to change your logged disk drive, you can load the text file along with WordStar by typing **WS EXAMPLE.1** after the CP/M prompt.

```
CP/M VER.2.2

A>WS EXAMPLE.1 ◄—— Press RETURN
```

Now appearing on the screen is Example 1 as you last saved it.

Saving (^K)

<8.05>
[3-11]
There are four save commands. Why do you need four ways to save a file? All of the material that is placed on the disk is referred to as a file, whether it is something you typed into the computer and saved, like Example 1, or a complicated commercial program like WordStar. Let's consider each of the save commands and see when they are appropriate.

^**KD** — Done edit. When you have finished a letter, document, or other material and want to continue using WordStar or print the material, use this command. It will save your file and return you to the WordStar main menu.

^**KS** — Save and reedit. Using this command saves what you have entered on the disk and returns you to your document file so that you may continue. When you are working on a particularly long piece of material, you should save what you have typed about every 20 or 25 minutes so that in case of a power failure or other mishap you will not lose completed work.

^**KX** — Save and exit. This command saves the file you are working on and returns you to the operating system (CP/M).

^**KQ** — Abandon edit. Suppose for some reason you decide the editing you are doing is not acceptable, and you would rather have your original version of the file than the corrections you just made on the screen. Type ^**KQ** and all of your corrections will be ignored. Load your original file again from your disk.

Printing (P or ^KP)

<11.1>
[8-8]
Once you've finished entering a document, you may want to print it out on paper. From the previous section you know that you should type ^**KD** to save material typed into WordStar. The menu will appear and you should select **P** to print a file. When you type **P** you will be presented with a series of questions. These questions, and the proper responses, are listed below.

NAME OF FILE TO PRINT?

Enter the name of the file as it appears in the directory. You may use either upper- or lower-case letters.

DISK FILE OUTPUT (Y/N):

To print on your printer, press RETURN or **N** for the No answer. To "print" to another disk file, type **Y,** and follow the instructions in the Micropro manual. RETURN is the default response for each of these questions.

START AT PAGE NUMBER (RETURN for Beginning)?

If you wish to start somewhere other than page 1, indicate the appropriate page number. Enter 1 or RETURN to start on page 1.

STOP AFTER PAGE NUMBER (RETURN for End)?

Again indicate the appropriate page number.

USE FORMFEEDS (Y/N):

If using single sheets of paper, or if your printer does not have a "top of form" setting, you will not want to use formfeeds. Enter **N.** Be sure to use dot commands to set paper length.

If using continuous-form paper, and your printer has a "top of form" setting, it will be faster and more accurate to enter **Y** and use the formfeed option.

SUPPRESS PAGE FORMATTING (Y/N):

Press RETURN or **N** unless you wish to show the formatting commands. (See Example 13C for illustration.)

PAUSE FOR PAPER CHANGE BETWEEN PAGES (Y/N):

Press RETURN when using continuous paper. When working with single sheets of paper, press **Y** or **N** so that you may insert a new sheet of paper for each page.

READY PRINTER, HIT RETURN:

Before responding to this question by pressing RETURN, be sure the paper in the printer is adjusted properly.

Suppose you have just printed out a four-page document and discovered something on page 3 that must be corrected. You return to

WordStar, load your document, make the necessary corrections, and save the program by typing ^**KD**. The main menu now appears, and you press **P** to print a file. Enter the name of the file, and press RETURN in response to the questions until the question START AT PAGE NUMBER? appears; then type **3**. Press RETURN for the remaining questions.

Notice that while a file is printing, the message after the P on the menu is STOP PRINT. To stop the printer, press **P**. The printer will stop within a few lines. You will then be given a choice of "Y" ABANDON PRINT, "N" TO RESUME, or "^U" TO HOLD. Notice also that the message PRINT PAUSED now appears in the status line. In this case the appropriate response is **Y**; it will return you to the no-file menu.

```
P   PRINT PAUSED   printing EXAMPLE.1   editing no file

    "Y" TO ABANDON PRINT, "N" TO RESUME, ^U TO HOLD: Y
```

You can also print a file while you are editing another file. To do this, type ^**KP** while you are editing a document file. WordStar will display the same print menu to set up the print function. While a file is printing, you can continue editing.

Other File Commands:
Rename (E), Copy (O), Delete (Y)

There are three other file commands which can be accessed from the no-file menu.

[1-9]   **E** — Rename a File. Use this option to change the name of a disk file. Pressing **E** presents you with the question

NAME OF FILE TO RENAME?

Enter the name EXAMPLE.1, press RETURN. You now have the question

NEW NAME?

Enter the name EXAMPLE.X, press RETURN.

Notice that the name on the directory has changed. You would now load your original EXAMPLE.1 text by entering the filename EXAMPLE.X. WordStar will not allow you to change the name to that of a file already on the disk. Change the name back to the original, since we will refer to EXAMPLE.1 in later lessons.

[1-9] **O** — Copy a File. This option allows you to copy a file from one disk to another or to copy a file onto the same disk under another name.

Pressing **O** presents you with the question

NAME OF FILE TO COPY FROM?

When you enter a filename and press RETURN, WordStar asks

NAME OF FILE TO COPY TO?

If you enter a filename that already exists, WordStar will ask "OVERWRITE Y/N?". If you respond yes, the existing file will be replaced.

[1-10] **Y** — Delete a File. Press **Y** and you are asked

NAME OF FILE TO DELETE?

Use this option to delete any file which appears on your disk directory. You will use this command frequently to rid your disk of files you no longer need.

With each of these file commands you may, of course, precede your filename with a disk drive option (for example, B:EXAMPLE.1).

EXERCISES

1. Save the file you have in the computer and type in Example 3. Name the file EXAMPLE.3. Type the entire example and then use the cursor controls to go back and correct any errors.

2. Use EXAMPLE.3 to practice changing the spacing, scrolling, changing the ruler line, and reforming the paragraphs.

3. Save the file and print it. (When editing a file, be sure to save it before printing. The material printed is the last version of your file saved on the disk.)

EXAMPLE 3

Memo to: Bill Smith

From: John Regal

Some of the computer projects we are now working on will require time to complete after the close of the school year this June and prior to the opening of school in September.

The projects are:

1.   Martinez Elementary class lists and State Attendance Reports

2.   Las Juntas class lists and State Attendance Reports

3.   Attendance register for Special Education

With these, and additional pending assignments in mind, I would like to discuss with you compensation for myself and a clerical assistant to handle this workload outside the regular school year.

JR/ljp

March 5, 1981

Tabs
Ruler Line
Centering
Margin Release

<u>LESSON 4</u>

You have already been introduced to the ruler line. When you begin editing a document, its left and right ends are set to certain values by WordStar. These values are column 1 for the left end and 65 for the right end. Initial tabs are also set.

Tab (^I)

[3-8]   To move to the next tab stop, enter ^I. If your INSERT ON message is on the screen, you can insert blank text spaces up to the next tab stop by using this ^I tab command.

If your terminal has a TAB key, you may be able to use it instead of ^I.

Ruler Line (^OF)

<7.3>
{7.4}
[2-12]
Besides setting the left and right ends of the ruler line as you did in Lesson 2, you may also do so by typing in the first line of the material with which you are working, then placing the cursor at the beginning of that line and pressing ^OF.

Try this by starting a sentence in column 6, and continuing until the cursor is in column 66. Move the cursor to the first letter of the sentence and press ^OF. Notice how the ruler line has changed its length. You may use this method of setting the ruler line for material just typed in, or you may set the ruler line to the length of any line that is on the screen.

Tab Stops (!)

<8.06>
[3-8]
Sometimes the default tab settings are not appropriate for the material being entered. We will now set up a special ruler line with tabs in columns 20, 40, and 60. The ruler line should extend from column 2 to column 78. Place the cursor in column 2 and type dashes (not underlines) until the cursor is in column 20, then type an exclamation point. The exclamation point represents a tab setting. Continue in this manner with dashes and exclamation points in the appropriate columns until the cursor is in column 79 (the last dash is in 78). Now place the cursor at the first dash (column 2) and press ^OF. The ruler line and tabs have changed to conform to this new model.

Decimal Tabs (#)

{8.06}
[4-14]
The same procedure you used in the previous section to set ordinary tab stops can also be used to set decimal tabs. In the model for the ruler line you just typed, move the cursor over the exclamation mark in column 60 and type # (number sign) to replace the exclamation mark. Move the cursor to the first dash of the line again and press ^OF; the ruler line has changed and the exclamation mark in column 60 becomes a # sign.

To see how this works, press RETURN so that the cursor is in the line below the ruler line model and press TAB (or ^ I) three times. Notice that when the cursor moved to column 60, the message "Decimal Tab" appeared in the status line. Now watch the screen and type in the number $1,240.49. As the $1,240 is typed in, the cursor stays in the same position and characters just entered force the previously entered characters to the left. Now enter the decimal. It takes the position of the cursor, which moves to the right. Notice also that the "Decimal Tab" message no longer appears in the status line. Further entry will take place in the normal manner.

Nonprinting Ruler Line

{8.06}   The model just typed in for the ruler line is in your file. If the file is
[4-14]   saved and printed, this ruler line will also be printed. If you won't need this ruler line again, it can be deleted (deleting is discussed in Lesson 5). In most cases it's better to keep it in your file as a nonprinting line. Sometimes you will have three or four nonprinting models for the ruler line in a file so that you can quickly change it without having to retype the model. To make the ruler line model nonprinting, place the cursor in column 1 of the ruler line and turn insert on (^V), type two periods, then type ^P and press RETURN. Then turn insert off (^V again). This line can be seen on the screen, and it will be saved in the file on the disk, but it will not show up when you print the file.

Centering (^OC)

<8.06>   Take a look at Example 4. It requires centering text at the top of the
[4-6]   page and using two different line lengths. In addition, the numbers 1, 2, 3, 4 are printed outside the margins in the middle portion of the letter.

The first exercise in this lesson asks you to type in the letter provided. Abandon or save whatever is in the computer now. Start a new file and name it EXAMPLE.4. For the main part of the example letter we will use the default ruler line. Start with the cursor in column 1, line 1, and type in **STRANDS HIGH SCHOOL**. Now press ^OC and the material typed in will be centered within the ruler line. Press RETURN to end the line, and enter the next three lines, using ^OC to center each line of text.

Enter the body of the letter, pressing RETURN only when you want to enter a blank line or end a paragraph.

Margin Release (^OX)

To enter the list of requirements in Example 4, we need a new ruler line. The easiest way to do this is to use the space bar to move the cursor to column 5. Begin the first sentence. When you have finished the word "high" at the right end of the line, do not press RETURN, but use the cursor controls to move the cursor to the "T" at the beginning of the line, and press ^OF. The ruler line has changed. Type ^OX, and the message MAR REL will appear in the status line. Move the cursor to the left and type in the **1**. Now move to the right end of the line by pressing ^QD, and continue typing the rest of the sentence. Insert the blank line before requirement 2. Now we have a problem. If you just type a **2** it will move inside the left margin, which is not where you want it. Type ^OX (margin release); notice that the message MAR REL appears in the status line; now type the **2** and the period, type ^OX to turn off the margin release, and continue typing in the second requirement. Use the same procedure for requirements 3 and 4. When you have finished requirement 4, reset the ruler line to the original value. To do this, return to a line of proper length, type ^OF, return to the bottom of the file (^OC), and finish the letter. Use the TAB key to quickly move the cursor to the proper position for the salutation and the name.

A word of caution: if you have to make corrections and it will be necessary to reform a paragraph (^B), be sure that you have the ruler line set properly for that paragraph.

If you reform any of the paragraphs that have numbers outside the ruler line, be sure to place the cursor to the right of the numbers before you press ^B; otherwise they will be moved to conform to the ruler line.

Paragraph Tab (^OG)

{8.06} Paragraph tab allows you to temporarily reset your left margin. Pressing
[4-1]   ^OG once sets the left margin to the first tab stop. Each successive

pressing of ^**OG** moves the ruler line one additional tab stop to the right. If your terminal supports reverse video, the ruler line will indicate the position of the new left margin. If you don't have reverse video, your ruler line will remain unchanged. When you begin entering or editing text within that paragraph, you'll see that the tab-related left margin is in effect.

The most common use of paragraph tab is to reform indented questions or paragraphs. The ruler line automatically returns to the original left margin after a RETURN, or after you reform a paragraph or move the cursor to a new paragraph.

EXERCISES

1. Type in the letter in Example 4. It has sections requiring two or more ruler lines of different lengths. Make up a model for each and make it nonprinting. Print out the file to be sure these ruler line models do not print.

2. Practice with some additional material which requires centering. Change the length of the ruler line and recenter the words on the new ruler line.

3. Practice with some material that requires you to type in something outside the margins. Reform a paragraph that has something outside the left margin.

EXAMPLE 4

37

STRANDS HIGH SCHOOL
Career Center
150 Main Street
San Diego, California

Dear Student Employer:

Please be advised that one of our students who has been employed by you has applied for credit in the Outside Work Experience Program.

We would like to acquaint you with the basic requirements of this program so that there is no misunderstanding at a later date.

Requirements

1. The student must be regularly enrolled in the high school for no less than a minimum day, which consists of three classes.

2. Absence from school automatically is considered absence from the Outside Work Experience job station. It is generally considered that if a student cannot attend school, he cannot go to work.

3. A student cannot be employed in excess of eight hours per day, including school time.

    Example

    If a student has four classes in the morning, and works four hours after school, he is within the requirements. However, if a student has a full class schedule, he will be entitled to work four hours after school.

4. All students under the age of eighteen must have a duly issued work permit.

I hope this letter is informative and that you and your employee will be able to comply. We would like to express our appreciation for your cooperation. If you have any questions, please call me at 932-8976.

Yours very truly,

JOHN SMITH

Setting and Clearing Tabs
Deleting
Inserting

Tab Set (^OI)

<8.06>
[4-1]

You have already used the tabs in the default ruler line and set your own tabs with exclamation marks. We will now discuss yet another method of setting tabs.

Type ^OI and WordStar will ask at which column number you wish to set the tab. Enter the appropriate column number, press RETURN, and notice that an exclamation mark appears in that column on the ruler line. Or press the ESCAPE key, and the current cursor column, indicated in the status line, will be entered for the tab stop.

Try this with a new ruler line. Create a ruler line beginning at column 2 and ending at column 77, with no tabs. Using ^OI, place tab stops at columns 27 and 52. No tab stop is needed in column 2 since word wrap will automatically start you at the beginning of the ruler line.

Press RETURN and the cursor will be in line 1, column 1. Type in your name. The name, of course, will begin in column 2, under the left edge of the ruler line. Press the TAB key and the cursor will move to column 27 under the first tab symbol on the ruler line; type in another name and move the cursor back to the first letter of that name.

Use this ruler line to type in the names from Example 5A. Save the file.

Tab Clear (^ON)

{8.06}
[4-1]

Type ^ON and WordStar will ask "Which column number to clear the tab?" or "A for all." Enter a column number to clear a tab in that column; enter **A** to clear all tabs. Pressing ESCAPE clears a tab in the current cursor column, indicated in the status line.

Deleting (^Y)

<8.04>
[3-10]

There are two ways to delete small amounts of text. One method deletes an entire line of text and closes up the line space where that text was once placed. The second method blanks characters on a line but does not delete the line space.

To delete an entire line and its space, place the cursor anywhere on the line and press ^Y. To try this on the names and addresses you just entered, place the cursor to the left of the name in the first line and type ^Y; all three names on that line are deleted, and line 2 becomes line 1.

To delete characters on a line, use ^QY. To try this, place the cursor to the right of the first street address and type ^QY; the street addresses to the right of the cursor are gone. To erase an entire line, just place the cursor at the beginning of the line and press ^QY.

There are other delete keys and commands that you should know. They are

^G   Delete the character under the cursor.

^Q[DELETE key]   Delete text on the line to the left of the cursor (similar to ^QY).

[DELETE key]   If you have this key on your keyboard, it will delete one character at a time to the left of the cursor.

^T   Delete an entire word at a time (reads to the next period or space), always to the right of the cursor.

Practice using all of these delete commands.

Inserting (^V)

[2-10]   You may have already seen the INSERT ON message printed on the status line when you started up WordStar. The ^V command controls whether insert is on or off. If insert is on, press ^V and it will be turned off; the INSERT ON message on the status line also will be turned off. Press ^V again and insert will be turned on.

When insert is on, any character you type in will be entered to the left of the cursor, and all text following the inserted character will be moved to the right. You can insert characters, tab spaces, and entire lines. To insert a blank line, place the cursor at the left margin of the line which should follow the blank line, then press RETURN.

To add words to a paragraph, you will likely use the insert and reform paragraph commands. To illustrate, let's add a few words to our text in EXAMPLE.1.

```
                     microprocessors and
     Most  applications  of ʌmicroprocessing in  our schools have
been on a very small scale and, it seems to me, that what we need
at the  moment is demonstration of specific  benefits which might
be realized from the purchase and installation of microcomputers.
```

Move the cursor to the beginning of the word "microprocessing," press ^V to turn insert on, then type the desired insert. When you've finished entering the insert, press ^V to turn insert off. Notice the text is extending past the right margin where you inserted text.

```
     Most applications of microprocessors and microprocessing in our schools have
been on a very small scale  and, it seems to me, that what we need
at the moment is demonstration of specific benefits which might
be realized from  the  purchase and installation of microcomputers.
```

With the cursor still on the first line, press ^**B** to reform the paragraph. WordStar will adjust the text to the margins again.

```
     Most applications of microprocessors and microprocessing in
our schools have been on a very small scale and, it seems to me,
that what we need at the moment is demonstration of specific
benefits which might be realized from the purchase and
installation of microcomputers.
```

You will use the insert and delete commands frequently as you edit and correct files. Don't forget to use ^**B** to reform paragraphs as needed.

EXERCISES

1. Add six names and addresses to those you already entered in this lesson. Practice deleting with this file. Be sure you can quickly delete left, right, or middle names without disturbing those you don't wish to delete.

2. Type in Example 5B. Set up your ruler line with decimal tabs in the appropriate positions before you enter any material.

3. You now have all the commands necessary for efficient editing of a document. Starting with EXAMPLE.1 proofread and correct any errors in the examples previously entered and saved.

EXAMPLE 5A

Veronica Lopez 520 Ridgeville Drive San Jose, CA 94395	Mark Jones 872 Olivet Road Alma, IL 98432	Lisa Maxwell 956 Bristol Road Lyman, WA 59874
Mary Lewis 120 Colgate Road Steele, MI 65753	Sam Parker 754 Alameda Drive Downey, ID 45634	Julie Rogers 504 Sucrest Lane Alto, TX 59735
Susie Waldo 2321 Brisbon Lane Shook, MI 46843	Johnny O'Brien 483 Virginia Street Chula, GA 28723	Greg Saunders 384 Sunset Road Lott, TX 96746

EXAMPLE 5B

| | Year Ended December 80 | |
	1980	1979
Sales, less returns and allowances	$89,731,224	$81,427,649
Other income	743,012	677,111
Total revenues	90,474,236	82,104,760
Costs and expenses		
Cost of goods sold	68,447,490	60,251,113
Selling, general and administrative expenses	15,096,582	13,934,940
Other expenses	766,831	737,417
State and Federal income taxes	3,005,624	3,760,089
Total costs and expenses	87,316,527	78,683,559
Net income before extraordinary items of income or expense	3,157,709	3,421,201
Add or (deduct) extraordinary items of income or expense (net of related income tax $367,807)	(385,862)	-
Net income	$2,771,847	$ 3,421,201
Earnings per share of common stock:		
Earnings before extraordinary item	$1.34	$1.44
Extraordinary item	.16	-
Net earnings	$1.18	$1.44

Special Print Functions

To get started with the print functions, open a file and type in Example 6A.

Boldface (^PB)

<10.1> Place the cursor over the first letter of the word "print" in the first line,
[7-1]   turn insert on (^V), and type ^PB. Move the cursor immediately after
        the "s" in "functions" and with insert still on, again type ^PB. The
        words "print functions" are now bracketed by the symbols ^B. The
        screen can't show boldface, so these symbols are to let you know that
        these words will be in boldface when the document is printed. Notice
        also that on the screen this line extends past the right end of the ruler
        line, but since the ^B's will not be printed out, your printed document
        will still be right-justified. Move the cursor a few spaces to the left of the
        words "print functions" and, with the cursor controls, move the cursor

one space at a time to the right. Watch the column number in the status line and notice that it does not change when the cursor crosses the ^B symbols. If you have doubts about what column a number or letter is in because of these control symbols in a line, you can always check the column number in the status line.

Print the file to check the right justification and appearance of the boldface.

Additional Print Functions (^PS, ^PD, ^PX, ^PV, ^PT)

<10.1>
[7-1]
Five print functions are listed below. Practice using these functions now, entering the command characters before and after the text you want to be affected. Use the same file and print it so you can again check the right justification and appearance of the text.

Underscore (^PS)	Underlines a word or group of words.
Double strike (^PD)	Makes a word or phrase stand out; not as dark as boldface.
Strikeout (^PX)	Strikeout is used as indicated in this example: S̶t̶r̶i̶k̶e̶o̶u̶t̶.
Subscript (^PV)	Subscript can be used in math equations.
Superscript (^PT)	Superscript is convenient to use with math equations or to indicate footnotes.

Not all printers are capable of handling all of the WordStar special print functions. Check the manual for your printer if you have difficulty with any of these functions.

There are some additional print functions that are not used as often as the ones just described. We will discuss them now, since you may want to use them at some point.

Print Pause (^PC)

<10.1>
[7-2]
^C can be placed anywhere in a file so that the printing will stop precisely where you want it to. You can then change print wheels to get special characters or italics for a word or phrase. A ^C must be placed at the end

of this section so the printer will again stop, enabling you to reinsert the original daisy wheel. When the printer stops, PRINT PAUSED will appear in the status line; typing **P** will restart the printer.

Ribbon Color (^PY)

<10.1>
[7-2]
If in your work you use a red-black ribbon, you can control what will be printed in red by typing ^**PY** before and after the section you wish in red. On the screen the section will be bracketed by the symbols ^Y.
    Caution: Be sure the switch under the ribbon cartridge is set for red-black. If you switch back to multi-strike ribbon, be sure the switch is in the proper position or you will get only half the use you should from your ribbon.

Alternate Pitch (^PA)

[7-3]
When printing wide text, you should experiment with condensed print if your printer has that option. You may be able to select an alternate pitch, such as condensed print, on your printer by using the ^**PA** command in your file. Return to normal pitch by entering ^**PN**.
    Lesson 13 discusses working with long lines.

Print Display On/Off (^OD)

{8.06}
[4-4]
If you have several of the special print functions inserted in your text, it is sometimes difficult to visualize the appearance of the printed document because of the display of the nonprinting control characters. Fortunately, WordStar allows you to turn these control characters off. Press ^**OD**; the control characters no longer display, and the position of the characters on the screen will be the same as when printed. Press ^**OD** again and the control characters will reappear. Be sure the control characters are displayed when you are editing a file so that you are aware of their position.
    In addition to eliminating the display of control characters, ^**OD** also eliminates the display of hyphens that do not print.

EXERCISES

1. Type in Example 6B using the appropriate print functions so that when you print it out the appearance is the same as that of the Example.

2. Edit the exercise you typed in for Lesson 4, changing the high school name and address to boldface and the words ''Requirements'' and ''Example'' to double strike.

The print functions are listed near the bottom of the command sheet. In some documents they are not only necessary but, when used appropriately, give your work a very professional appearance.

EXAMPLE 6B

Mr. Bob Harris

AV INVENTORY - SCHOOL CODE

As you requested, the following is school identification by code.

                    1..........Martinez Elementary

                    2..........John Swett

                    3..........Las Juntas

                    4..........Martinez Junior High

                    5..........District Office

                    6..........Adult School

                    7..........Trailer

                    8..........Alhambra High School

Move and Copy Block Commands

Block commands allow you to perform several functions that are not possible with a standard typewriter. Rather than work with single characters, words, or even lines of text, with blocks you can manipulate larger sections of text.

Moving Blocks (^KB, ^KK, ^KV)

<8.09>
[6-4]
Load your EXAMPLE.1 file. Turn insert on. Place the cursor at the beginning of the file over the "M" in "Most," then type ^**KB**. The symbols <B> appear on the screen and "Most" will have moved three spaces to the right, but the status line shows the "M" remaining in column 1. Move the cursor to the end of the first paragraph, after the period, and type ^**KK**. The symbols <K> appear after the period. You have now *blocked off* a paragraph. (On some display terminals, blocks appear as dimmer text, and the <B> and <K> characters are not displayed.)

Move the cursor to the end of the file (^**QC**) and press RETURN. Type ^**KV** and the blocked off paragraph is moved to where the cursor is positioned.

Place the cursor back at the beginning of the file and again type ^**KV**. The paragraph is returned to its original position. With this command you can move a phrase, sentence, paragraph, or page to any position in the document. Just place the cursor in the position where you want the blocked material to be placed and type ^**KV**. Try this now by interchanging paragraphs 1 and 2. A block remains defined until another block is specified.

There are limitations as to how large the blocked material you wish to move can be, depending on the amount of memory available in the computer. If you try to move too large a block, you will be informed by the message BLOCK TOO LONG. You can then reblock it into two or three smaller sections and move them one at a time.

Copy Block (^KC)

<8.09>
[6-4]

Instead of moving a block of material from one place to another, you may want to copy some text but not have it removed from its original position. To do this, block off the material in the same manner you did above, move the cursor to the position for the new text, and type ^**KC**. This copies the blocked material at the position of the cursor and also leaves the material in its original position.

To block off a different section, move the cursor to the beginning of the new section and type ^**KB**, then move it to the end of the section and type ^**KK**. The symbols <B> and <K> now bracket the new section and no longer appear in the previous block. You can change the blocked section as often as you like.

In order to eliminate the symbols <B> and <K> from the screen display, type ^**KH**. The symbols can no longer be seen, but are still in the file. Type ^**KH** again and they will reappear — try it.

Blocking Columns On/Off (^KN)

[6-4]

With WordStar 3.x, you can mark blocks within columns, not just lines of text (versions 1.x and 2.x cannot do this). Press ^**K** and, from the menu displayed, choose the option N. This changes the block moving capabilities of WordStar to column mode.

Enter the first portion of Example 7C. (*Note:* Enter only the first row and use the block commands to copy in the next four rows.) Now using column mode, move the columns to duplicate the pattern in section (2) of the example. You can do this with two block moves. Work with this example to create the other patterns shown.

You can move or copy not only columns of characters but also columns of spaces, as was done in section (4) of this example. This can be a very useful application when you have a long file with columns of names or numbers and you wish to change the spacing. To do this, block off a long column of spaces, deleting or copying them to the new position.

EXERCISES

1. Type in five names and addresses with different ZIP codes (one name per line).

2. Using the block commands, rearrange the names and addresses so they are in alphabetical order.

3. Rearrange the names and addresses so they are in order by ZIP code from smallest to largest.

4. Enter Example 7A. Using block commands, arrange the questions in reverse order.

5. Enter Example 7B. Forms of one type or another are easy to make with WordStar by using the block commands. Set the ruler line and tabs to conform to this Example and enter the form as far as the B on the right-hand side. (Do not enter the A or B.) With the cursor in the position of the B, type ^KK. Move the cursor to the position of the A in the Example and type ^KB. Move the cursor to the end of the file (the position of C) and type ^KC. Move the cursor back to position A and again type ^KB, then return to the end of the file and type ^KC. By repeating this process you will move progressively larger blocks of material. Keep an eye on the line number in the status line so that you don't go past the end of the page.

PHYSICS TEST

Chapters 7-8

Name_____   Period_____

1. If a small planet were discovered whose distance from the sun
    was sixteen times that of the earth, how many times longer
    would it take to circle the sun?

    _____

2. The radius of the moon's orbit is 60 times greater than the
    radius of the earth. How many times greater is the
    acceleration of a falling body on the earth than the
    acceleration of the moon toward the earth?

    _____

3. At what height above the earth's surface will a rocket have
    1/4 the force of gravitation on it that it would have at sea
    level? Express your answer in earth radii.

    _____

4. A 75-kg boy stands 1 meter away from a 65-kg girl. Calculate
    the force of attraction (gravitational) between them.

    _____

5. You push a body with a force of 4 newtons for 1/2 sec. What
    impulse do you give the body?

    _____

6. What average force is necessary to stop a hammer with 25
    newton-sec momentum in 0.05 sec?

    _____

7. What happens to the momentum of a car when it comes to a stop?

    _____

8. What is the kinetic energy of a 2-kg hammer moving at 20
    m/sec?

    _____

EXAMPLE 7B

COMPUTER CENTER LOG

JOB DESCRIPTION	IN-DATE	FROM	OUT-DATE	TO

EXAMPLE 7C

```
(1)
AAAAA   BBBBB   CCCCC   11111   22222   33333
AAAAA   BBBBB   CCCCC   11111   22222   33333
AAAAA   BBBBB   CCCCC   11111   22222   33333
AAAAA   BBBBB   CCCCC   11111   22222   33333
AAAAA   BBBBB   CCCCC   11111   22222   33333

(2)
11111   22222   33333   AAAAA   BBBBB   CCCCC
11111   22222   33333   AAAAA   BBBBB   CCCCC
11111   22222   33333   AAAAA   BBBBB   CCCCC
11111   22222   33333   AAAAA   BBBBB   CCCCC
11111   22222   33333   AAAAA   BBBBB   CCCCC

(3)
11111   AAAAA   22222   BBBBB   33333   CCCCC
11111   AAAAA   22222   BBBBB   33333   CCCCC
11111   AAAAA   22222   BBBBB   33333   CCCCC
11111   AAAAA   22222   BBBBB   33333   CCCCC
11111   AAAAA   22222   BBBBB   33333   CCCCC

(4)
11111      AAAAA      22222      BBBBB      33333      CCCCC
11111      AAAAA      22222      BBBBB      33333      CCCCC
11111      AAAAA      22222      BBBBB      33333      CCCCC
11111      AAAAA      22222      BBBBB      33333      CCCCC
11111      AAAAA      22222      BBBBB      33333      CCCCC
```

Read, Write, and Delete Block Commands Set Marks

The previous lesson covered the most frequently used block commands, but others are occasionally useful. These are described below.

Delete Block (^KY)

<8.09> Load in Example 7A and block off question 3. Type ^KY and the entire
[6-5]   block is deleted. This is an easy way to delete large sections of material.

Write Block (^KW)

<8.09> This command is used to write a block of material to the disk. Suppose
[6-5]   you have a paragraph or section of a report that is to be used in several
        different documents. The first time you type it in, block it off and type

^**KW**; WordStar will respond with NAME OF FILE TO WRITE TO. You type in the name and press RETURN, and the blocked material will be saved on the disk. The file name you use must be that of a new file. If you use a name already on disk, WordStar will replace that file with the blocked material.

Read File (^KR)

<8.09>
[6-6]
This command is used to take material from the disk and add it to the file you are editing. In this case, you place the cursor wherever you want to add the material from the disk; type ^**KR**, and WordStar will ask for the name of the disk file. After you supply the name, press RETURN, and the material from the disk will be inserted in the file you are editing at the position of the cursor. Your disk file is left intact.

Let's try this now with one of the questions from Example 7A. Block off a question. Type ^**KW**, enter a new file name, and press RETURN. Type ^**KY** to delete the question from the file you are editing. To put the question back, place the cursor where you want the question to appear, type ^**KR**, and type the file name under which you saved the question. The question is back in place.

Delete File (^KJ)

<8.09>
[6-7]
To clear the disk of unnecessary files, we will get rid of the file used to save the question in the previous example. Type ^**KJ** and WordStar will ask for the name of the file you wish to delete. Give the name and press RETURN. Check the directory (type ^**KF**), and you will see that this file no longer appears. As long as you have the directory on the screen, note that there are several files with the extension (the part after the period) BAK. This occurs when you save a file more than once. The most recently edited version will have the name you gave it with the extension you gave it, if any. The previous version will have the extension BAK, which stands for *back-up*.

The delete file command can come in handy. Suppose you type in a long document, attempt to save it by typing ^**KD**, and get the message DISK FULL. This would be very frustrating if there weren't two

possible solutions. First, check the directory and see if there are a few
back-up files you can delete, or perhaps a file that is no longer needed
(but don't exit to the no-file menu to do this). If there are unneeded
files, use ^**KJ** to get rid of them. The second possibility is to place a disk
with plenty of space in another drive, block off your file, and write it to
the other drive. To do this, use the prefix for the new drive on the name
of the file. If it is a long file you may need to use ^**KW** more than once.
Be sure to use a different file name each time you write a block to the
disk.

Of course, the easiest thing to do is check your disk before you start,
making sure that there is sufficient room for your file.

Set Marks (^K0-9)

<8.08>
[5-1]
In documents of several pages it is useful to set *marks* at appropriate
intervals so that you may quickly go to any part of the document. Ten of
these marks can be set (0-9). Although it is not particularly useful with a
short file, we will try it with Example 7A. There is no point in putting a
mark at the beginning or end of a file since you already have commands
to go to these positions. Place the first mark at question 1. Place the
cursor in column 1 on this line and type ^**K0**. The symbols <0> will
appear. Move the cursor to question 2, column 1, and type ^**K1**.
Continue in this manner so that you have the appropriate symbols next
to each question.

Now when you type ^**Q** and one of the integers 0 through 9, the
cursor will return to the proper mark. This procedure is most useful for
long documents.

EXERCISES

1. Load in text from Example 1. Block off the first half and write it to the disk. Do the same with the second half (using a new name).

2. Using the block read command, join these two files together again.

3. Using the delete file command, delete the two previously created files from the disk.

4. Delete all back-up and other unwanted files from your disk. (Be sure to keep one copy of each Example.)

Print Height, Width,
And Length
Dot Commands

Without knowing it, you have been using the *dot commands* since you first started using WordStar. Dot commands control many different print specifications. The "dot" referred to is actually a period.

Before we discuss these commands, a brief review of a few basics will provide some background.

1. The most common paper size is 8 1/2 × 11 inches.
2. Typewriters print 10 or 12 characters per inch across the paper, 12 being the most common; 6 lines per inch are printed vertically.
3. On the screen you are working with 80 columns. In most cases not all of these columns are used for text, since the ruler line is usually set to a width less than 80.

In this lesson we will discuss four dot commands. Use the following chart for reference:

Command	Function	Default
.LH	Line Height (per inch)	8 (6 lines to the inch)
.CW	Character Width	12 (for standard pitch)
.PL	Paper Length	66 lines (11 inches)
.PO	Page Offset	8 columns (4/5 inch)

When entering any dot command the dot must be in column 1, followed by the two-letter command (either upper- or lower-case), a space, and finally the value, if required.

Line Height (.LH)

<10.2>
[7-9] This command allows you to specify how many lines per inch are printed on a page (some printers cannot be controlled this way—ask your printer representative if yours can). Line height is specified in units of 1/48 of an inch, and the default value is 8. Notice that 8/48 of an inch reduces to 1/6, or six lines per inch. All of the Examples you have printed so far have been printed at this default value.

Load the text from Example 3, and print it out at 8 lines per inch. To enter the line height dot command, you may have to insert a blank line at the beginning of the file. Type **.LH6**. Check the status line to be sure the dot is in column 1; note that you cannot have any file text in the same line as a dot command. The 6 tells you that the printer will scroll down 6/48, or 1/8, of an inch after each line is printed. Notice that when you move the cursor from the line with the dot command to the line below, the line number in the status line does not change. Save the file and print it out. Notice that the dot command does not print, and you now have 8 lines per inch.

Character Width (.CW)

<10.2>
[8-5] The base unit character width is 1/120 inch, a very small increment that allows some interesting effects. The default value is 12 (12/120 = 1/10), or 10 characters per inch. To change this value, type a period

in column 1, then **CW**, then a number representing the value you wish to use. **.CW10** (10/120 = 1/12) would be used to print 12 characters per inch. On some printers you cannot control the character width with the **.CW** command.

Paper Length (.PL)

<10.2>
[7-9]

Because the standard paper length is 11 inches and the printer normally prints 6 lines per inch, the default value here is 66. If you have paper of a nonstandard length or if you change the line height, you can change the number of lines that will print per page by entering that number after the **.PL** command.

Page Offset (.PO)

<10.2>
[7-11]

This command determines the left margin and has a default value of 8 (8/10, or 4/5, of an inch). This is appropriate in most cases, but when your file has particularly narrow or wide text this may need to be changed. Always use this command to control where a file is to be printed on the paper, rather than changing the position of the paper in the printer. Moving the paper and forgetting to return it to its original position is aggravating to the next user.

To practice with this command, load the text from Example 1. Change the ruler line so the left margin is in column 1 and the right margin is in column 50. Reform the paragraphs to conform to this ruler line. To print the file so it is centered on the paper, use the following guidelines. The paper is 8 1/2 inches, or 85 columns, wide. The text is 50 columns wide, so we have 85 − 50, or 35 columns to split between the left and right margins. Let's use 17 for the left margin, and 18 for the right. At the top of your file type **.PO 17** (remember, no other text should be placed on this line). Save and print the file.

EXERCISES

1. Example 9B shows display type printed from a WordStar file. Example 9A indicates what the file looks like when you enter it. Enter text as shown in Example 9A. Notice that the line height and character width were returned to their default values before the page offset command; this makes it easier to determine the correct value for the page offset. Print out the file, and compare it to Example 9B. (Remember, some printers cannot perform the **.LH** and **.LW** functions. For these printers, this example will not work.)

2. Change the character width and/or line height in the previous problem to get a different shape for the letter. Adjust the **.PO** command if necessary so the printout is uniform.

3. Create a file and print your initials in large letters. Use your imagination on the style for the letters; also try using a symbol other than =.

EXAMPLE 9A

```
.LH 2
.CW 4
=============                    =============
========= ====                  ==== =========
======== ====                    ==== ========
======== ====                     ==== ========
======== ====                    ==== ========
========   ====                  ==== ========
========   ====                ==== ========
========     =======           ========
========        ====           ========
========                       ========
========                       ========
========                       ========
========                       ========
========                       ========
========                       ========

                    ========                  ========
                    ========                  ========
                    ========                  ========
                    ========                  ========
                    ========                  ========
                    ========                  ========
                    ========                  ========
                    ========                  ========
                    ========                  ========
                    ========                  ========
                    ========                  ========
                    ========                  ========
                    ========                  ========
                    ========    ========================
                       ===============================
                       ===============================
                         ===========================
```

(continued)

```
.LH 8
.CW 12
.PO 29
.LH 2
.CW 4
```

```
          =================================
        =====================================
      =========================================
     ==========================================
     ========           ========
     ========
     ========
     ===================================
     ==================================
       ==================================
         ================================
                          ========
                          ========
     ========             ========
     ====================================
     =====================================
       ===================================
         =================================
```

```
              =====================================
              ======================================
              =======================================
              ========================================
              ========              ========
              ========              ========
              ========              ========
              ========              ========
              ========              ========
              ========              ========
              ========              ========
              ========              ========
              ========              ========
              ========              ========
              =========================================
              =======================================
              ======================================
              ====================================
```

(*continued*)

```
.LH 8
.CW 12




                ************************************
                C   A   T   A   L   O   G
                ************************************

                         ******
                         O   F
                         ******

                *************************************
                C   O   M   P   U   T   E   R
                *************************************


                *************************************
                P   R   O   G   R   A   M   S
                *************************************
```

EXAMPLE 9B

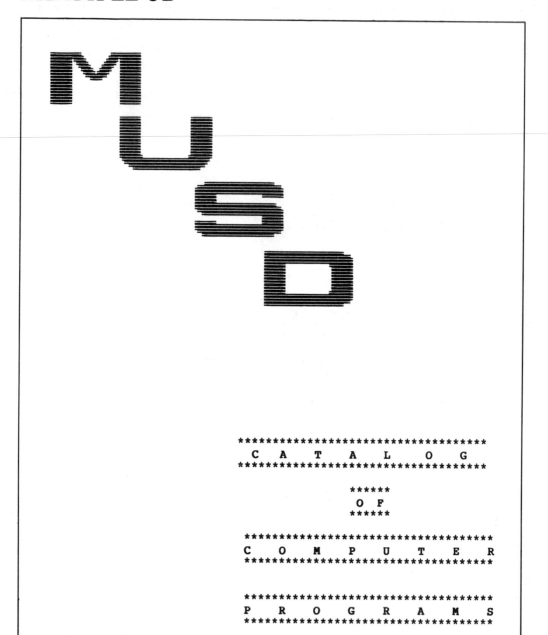

```
*************************************
C   A   T   A   L   O   G
*************************************

        *****
         O F
        *****

*************************************
C   O   M   P   U   T   E   R
*************************************


*************************************
P   R   O   G   R   A   M   S
*************************************
```

Heading and Footing
Dot Commands

In this lesson we will work with six more dot commands. The commands control what is printed at the top and bottom of each page. You should enter all of your dot commands at the beginning of the file, before entering any text. Use the following chart for reference:

Command	Function	Default
.MT	Margin Top	3 lines (1/2 inch)
.HM	Heading Margin	2 lines (1/3 inch)
.HE	Heading	Blank
.MB	Margin Bottom	8 lines (1 1/3 inch)
.FO	Footing	Page number unless other text added
.FM	Footing Margin (margin for page number)	2 lines (1/3 inch)

Margin Top (.MT)

<10.2>   .MT has a default value of 3 lines. Set your printer at the top of the
[7-9]   paper and let your text begin on line 1. When printing the file, the
           printer will scroll the paper up three lines before it begins to print. If this
           distance is not satisfactory, it can easily be changed by entering the
           number of lines to scroll after the .MT command. This value can be
           either more or less than the default value. Another way to control the
           top margin, particularly for single-page documents, is to insert blank
           lines at the top of the file.

Heading (.HE)

<10.2>   This command is used to place text at the top of each page of a printed
[8-2]   file. Any text typed after the .HE command will be printed at the top of
           each new page in your printout. You are limited to one line of heading
           text.

Heading Margin (.HM)

<10.2>   This command allows you to control the spacing between the heading
[7-10]   and the beginning of the file text. The value you give for the top margin
           (.MT) must be large enough to contain both the heading and the
           heading margin.

Margin Bottom (.MB)

<10.2>   Similar to the top margin command, this command allows you to specify
[7-9]   the number of lines to leave for a bottom margin. The default value is 8,
           or 1 1/3 inches. Occasionally you will want to reduce this value so that
           you can fit another line or two of text on the page. Enter this command
           at the beginning of your file.

Footing (.FO)

<10.2>   The manuscript page number is printed in this space, but you can use
[8-3]   this command to automatically print any information you like at the foot
of each page of your file. You are limited to one line of footing text.

Footing Margin (.FM)

<10.2>   This command determines the space between your file text and the page
[7-10]   number or footing text. Again, the spacing for the footing margin and
the footing text must be included in the bottom margin command.
There are three special format characters that can be used with the
heading (.HE) and footing (.FO) commands.

Prints the current page number in place of the symbol. In a
long document, the page number is automatically
incremented and prints in the position of the # symbol.

\   Prints the next character with no special interpretation (for
example, \ # will print # instead of the page number; \\ will
print \).

^K   Ignores following spaces up to the next character if the page
number is even. This is used to cause text or page numbers
to appear on the corner of the page farthest from the
binding.

EXERCISES

1. Use a ruler line with appropriate tabs to type in Example 10A. (Right margin is at 75.)

2. Use the dot commands to print your name and disk number in the heading. Print the page number in the footing in column 75.

3. Type in Example 10B. Print Example 10B with page numbers at the top of the page.

```
        VOCATIONAL EDUCATION STUDENT/COURSE INVENTORY

Student Name_____ Sex_____/_____
                                        (male)   (female)


Address_____ Telephone_____

        _____
              (city)

Grade Level_____ Birthdate_____/___/_____ LES Status_____
```

Disadvantaged Status   Racial/Ethnic Code   Handicapped Status
   DISAD.ST.   R/E CODE   HNDCAP ST.
-------------------   ------------------   --------------------

(EC)____Economic   (AI) ____American Indian (MR)____Mentally Retarded
(AC)____Academic   Alaskan Native (HH)____Hard of Hearing
                      (API)____Asian Pacific   (SI)____Speech Impaired
                                Islander   (VH)____Visually Handi-
                      (BNH)____Black,   capped
                                Non-Hispanic   (ED)____Emotionally Dis-
                      (H) ____Hispanic   turbed
                      (F) ____Filipino   (OHI)____Other Health Im-
                      (WNH)____White,   paired
                                Non-Hispanic   (MH)____Multi-handi-
                                                         capped
                                                (SLD)____Specific Learn-
                                                         ing Disabled

        VOCATIONAL EDUCATION PROGRAM PRESENTLY ENROLLED

I Office Occupations   II Industrial Arts
_____   _____
(AC)____Accounting & Computing Occupations (GM) ____General Metals
(FO)____Filing, Office Machines, Gen. Off. (VT) ____Voc.-Tech. Metals
(SS)____Stenographic,Secretarial,Related   (BA) ____Beg. Auto
(TO)____Typing & Related Occupations   (AA) ____Adv. Auto

                III Home Economics
                _____
        (CD) ____Child Development
        (SO) ____S.O.S/$ Sen.
        (H1) ____Hm. Ec. I
        (H2) ____Hm. Ec. II
        (AH) ____Adv. Hm. Ec.

EXAMPLE 10B

To: Mr. John Sears   Mr. Peter Sherwood
      Mr. Jack Evans   Mr. Pat Gena

From: Mr. Bob Harris

We have had discussions with several administrators of the
Martinez Unified School District during the past year concerning
projects to be implemented on the microcomputer. For example:

    Mike Lena   Audio-Visual Inventory
    Laura Foster   Elementary school testing
    Mary Aspen   High school proficiency tests
    Rich Laughlin   Elementary school attendance
    Bill Smith   Word Processing
    Jack Evans   Title I Management

Some of these projects are well underway; others are still in the
discussion stage.

The implementation of these requests has relied heavily on the
use of the ROP equipment, some of which is available for
administrative use approximately two hours each day.

Planning for these and future projects should be given careful
consideration by the administration. The main points to consider
are:

Hardware

We have at the high school now, or on order, the hardware to
implement these tasks at least at a minimal level.

The correcting of the elementary school tests with the inclusion
of data on each student and the Title I Management program will
probably exceed the capacity of our 5-1/4" disks; therefore,
consideration should be given to the purchase of a hard disk
(approximately $5,000).

Some of the projects (e.g., elementary school attendance, Title I
Management) would be more efficiently printed out on a high speed
printer (approximately $2,000).

When all of the above projects are on line along with others we
have been doing for some time, we will need full time use of at
least two terminals to obtain the output in a reasonable amount
of time. (The cost of an additional terminal will be between
$1,500 and $3,500 depending on some software information that
should be available before the end of the school year.)

(continued)

Software

There is also a variety of software required for the most efficient implementation of these projects.

The software should be compatible, not only for these projects, but also for those planned in the forseeable future (two or three years). It would also be cost effective to use the same software in the high school programming class, business classes, and for administrative word processing.

Facilities

Careful consideration should be given to housing the equipment required to perform these tasks. Because of the expense required for wiring and security, their location is not easily changed.

Since this cost can be considerable, the requirements to house this equipment, provide adequate, secure storage and have ample space for personnel in the foreseeable future should be taken into account.

Planning is also important for the optimum utilization of the equipment. It is important that some equipment not be placed where it is used only a small portion of the day while other equipment is overtaxed.

Easy access by the departments which make the most use of these facilities should be taken into account when locating this equipment.

Cost

The cost is, of course, vital. The District now spends in excess of $20,000 annually for computer related services. (It may be considerably more than this; Mr. Lena would have to determine the exact amount.)

The District has potential savings from at least three sources.

(1) Direct savings by having some of these outside services performed on District computers.

(2) Indirectly by using programs, such as the inventory program, which give better control over the audio-visual equipment thus saving some of the $6,000 in annual losses.

(3) By increasing efficiency with computer programs and word processing. Through attrition, some personnel would not have to be replaced.

(continued)

Of course, only through a careful study of District requirements
and current expenses for computer services could costs and
benefits be determined.

RH/ljp

January 13, 1981

Page and Page Number Dot Commands

LESSON 11

The remaining dot commands further control page numbering, page breaks, and comments not meant to be printed. Use the following chart for reference:

Command	Function
.OP	Omit the Page numbers
.PN	Page Numbers
.PC	Page number Column position (33 default)
.PA	New page
.CP	Conditional Page
.UJ	Microjustification
.BP	Bidirectional Print
.IG	Comment (Inserted on screen but not printed out)
..	Comment (Inserted on screen but not printed out)

81

Omit Page Numbers (.OP)

<10.2> You have probably noticed that on all files you have printed out so far,
[8-5] WordStar automatically printed out the page number. Typing **.OP** at the
beginning of your file will suppress the page numbering. Enter **.OP**
again to resume page number printing.

Page Number (.PN)

<10.2> This command allows you to set the first printing page number, and
[8-5] WordStar will automatically increment its page numbering from this
entry. If you wish to start the page numbering on some page other than
the first, type **.OP** on the first page and, at the top of the page where you
wish the numbering to start, type **.PN** and the first page number you
want. This is also used when documents are contained in two or more
files. Suppose file A has ten pages and file B, a continuation of A, has
seven. At the beginning of file B, type **.PN 11**. It will then begin at page
11 and number sequentially through page 17.

Page Number Column (.PC)

<10.2> Page numbers are normally centered at the bottom of the page. This
[7-10] command gives you a method of controlling the column in which the
page number is printed. Type **.PC** and the column number in which you
want the page number to appear. Remember that the # character,
described in the previous lesson, can be used in either the heading or
footing commands to indicate placement of a page number.

New Page (.PA)

<10.2> You have no doubt noticed that when your file has reached a certain
[7-11] length you get a series of dashes across the screen with a P in column 80.
The P is a flag character, and indicates where there will be a page break
when you print your file. This is very useful, but unfortunately it
doesn't always occur in the appropriate position. In long documents, or
documents with many charts or tables, you almost always have to

reposition this "page break." The **.PA** command allows you to force a page break at that line. To know where you need to force a page break, you might type in your entire document, then return to the beginning and scroll through the document, placing the **.PA** wherever you want a new page to begin. Never work from the end of the file to the beginning, or you may end up with a first page that is only a few lines long. Remember, you can add one to six lines of text to the page by changing the bottom margin.

Conditional Page (.CP)

<10.2>   A better way to avoid unwanted page breaks, but one that takes a little
[7-12]   getting used to, is the **.CP** n command, where n is the number of lines you specify should remain on the page. This allows you to go to the next page if there is not a specified number of lines left. Otherwise a new page is started. This command can be very useful, but it does take some practice for your document to come out correctly paged.

Microjustification (.UJ)

[8-7]   If your printer adjusts spaces proportionally, you will use the microjustification command frequently when printing out a file that contains tables or data in columns. If word wrap was on or a paragraph reform was applied in error, the file may appear correct on the screen, but when printed, the columns will not appear in perfect alignment. To eliminate this problem, enter the dot command **.UJ 0** before the table, and **.UJ 1** after the table. (**.UJ 0** turns microjustification off, and **.UJ 1** turns it back on.) The table will print just as it appears on the screen.

Bidirectional Print (.BP)

[8-7]   The command **.BP** allows you to turn bidirectional printing on or off. **.BP 0** turns it off and causes printing from left to right only. **.BP 1** turns it back on. If your printer does not use bidirectional print, it will not be affected by this command.

Ignore (.IG, ..)

<10.2>   This command allows you to insert remarks in your file that you can
[8-5]   read on the screen, but that are not printed. Two dots in the first two
         columns have the same effect.

---

1. Load the text from Example 1.
   a. Print the example without a page number.
   b. Print the page number in the heading instead of the footing.

2. With Example 1, practice changing the column of the page number in both heading and footing.

3. Type in and print out Example 11A. Note the use of character width commands. Example 11B shows the final appearance of the form.

4. Change the size of the printout by changing the **.CW** and **.LH** commands.

EXAMPLE 11A

```
.CW 7
.LH 4
```

```
.CW 10
```

	12:00	12:30	1:00	1:30	2:00	2:30	3:00	3:30	4:00	4:30	5:00	5:30	6:00	6:30	7:00
8:00	4.0	4.5	5.0	5.5	6.0	6.5	7.0	7.5	8.0	8.5	9.0				
8:30	3.5	4.0	4.5	5.0	5.5	6.0	6.5	7.0	7.5	8.0	8.5	9.0			
9:00	3.0	3.5	4.0	4.5	5.0	5.5	6.0	6.5	7.0	7.5	8.0	8.5	9.0		
9:30	2.5	3.0	3.5	4.0	4.5	5.0	5.5	6.0	6.5	7.0	7.5	8.0	8.5	9.0	
10:00	2.0	2.5	3.0	3.5	4.0	4.5	5.0	5.5	6.0	6.5	7.0	7.5	8.0	8.5	9.0
10:30	1.5	2.0	2.5	3.0	3.5	4.0	4.5	5.0	5.5	6.0	6.5	7.0	7.5	8.0	8.5
11:00	1.0	1.5	2.0	2.5	3.0	3.5	4.0	4.5	5.0	5.5	6.0	6.5	7.0	7.5	8.0
11:30	0.5	1.0	1.5	2.0	2.5	3.0	3.5	4.0	4.5	5.0	5.5	6.0	6.5	7.0	7.5
12:00		0.5	1.0	1.5	2.0	2.5	3.0	3.5	4.0	4.5	5.0	5.5	6.0	6.5	7.0
12:30			0.5	1.0	1.5	2.0	2.5	3.0	3.5	4.0	4.5	5.0	5.5	6.0	6.5
1:00				0.5	1.0	1.5	2.0	2.5	3.0	3.5	4.0	4.5	5.0	5.5	6.0
1:30					0.5	1.0	1.5	2.0	2.5	3.0	3.5	4.0	4.5	5.0	5.5
2:00						0.5	1.0	1.5	2.0	2.5	3.0	3.5	4.0	4.5	5.0
2:30							0.5	1.0	1.5	2.0	2.5	3.0	3.5	4.0	4.5
3:00								0.5	1.0	1.5	2.0	2.5	3.0	3.5	4.0

	12:00	12:30	1:00	1:30	2:00	2:30	3:00	3:30	4:00	4:30	5:00	5:30	6:00	6:30	7:00
8:00	4.0	4.5	5.0	5.5	6.0	6.5	7.0	7.5	8.0	8.5	9.0	9.5	—	—	—
8:30	3.5	4.0	4.5	5.0	5.5	6.0	6.5	7.0	7.5	8.0	8.5	9.0	—	—	—
9:00	3.0	3.5	4.0	4.5	5.0	5.5	6.0	6.5	7.0	7.5	8.0	8.5	9.0	—	—
9:30	2.5	3.0	3.5	4.0	4.5	5.0	5.5	6.0	6.5	7.0	7.5	8.0	8.5	9.0	—
10:00	2.0	2.5	3.0	3.5	4.0	4.5	5.0	5.5	6.0	6.5	7.0	7.5	8.0	8.5	9.0
10:30	1.5	2.0	2.5	3.0	3.5	4.0	4.5	5.0	5.5	6.0	6.5	7.0	7.5	8.0	8.5
11:00	1.0	1.5	2.0	2.5	3.0	3.5	4.0	4.5	5.0	5.5	6.0	6.5	7.0	7.5	8.0
11:30	0.5	1.0	1.5	2.0	2.5	3.0	3.5	4.0	4.5	5.0	5.5	6.0	6.5	7.0	7.5
12:00	—	0.5	1.0	1.5	2.0	2.5	3.0	3.5	4.0	4.5	5.0	5.5	6.0	6.5	7.0
12:30	—	—	0.5	1.0	1.5	2.0	2.5	3.0	3.5	4.0	4.5	5.0	5.5	6.0	6.5
1:00	—	—	—	0.5	0.1	1.5	2.0	2.5	3.0	3.5	4.0	4.5	5.0	5.5	6.0
1:30	—	—	—	—	0.5	1.0	1.5	2.0	2.5	3.0	3.5	4.0	4.5	5.0	5.5
2:00	—	—	—	—	—	0.5	1.0	1.5	2.0	2.5	3.0	3.5	4.0	4.5	5.0
2:30	—	—	—	—	—	—	0.5	1.0	1.5	2.0	2.5	3.0	3.5	4.0	4.5
3:00	—	—	—	—	—	—	—	0.5	1.0	1.5	2.0	2.5	3.0	3.5	4.0

Find and Replace
Commands

One of the most powerful features of any word processing system is the ability to find a given word or phrase in a file and automatically replace it with another word or phrase of your choice. Remember that another way to "find" a section of text easily is by using file markers (Lesson 8).

Find (^QF)

<8.07>
[5-2]

To begin this lesson, load in Example 4 and place the cursor at the beginning of the file. To initiate the find command type ^QF; WordStar will respond with FIND?. Your response can be any group of characters (*string*), partial word, word, or phrase up to 30 characters in length. For this exercise, type in the word **Example**, which occurs midway in the letter, and press RETURN. WordStar then responds with

OPTIONS? (?FOR INFO). For now, press RETURN (options will be discussed shortly).

```
^QF    A:EXAMPLE.1    PAGE 1 LINE 1 COL 01

       FIND? Example OPTIONS? (? FOR INFO)◄───Press RETURN
                                          └─────────────Press RETURN
```

WordStar searches through the file, starting from the cursor position, for the first occurrence of the word Example. If it finds the specified word, it will stop there. If it does not find the word Example by the time it reaches the end of the file, it will print a NOT FOUND message and ask you to press the ESCAPE key (this key is usually located above the CTRL key). After you press ESCAPE you can continue editing.

```
^QF    A:EXAMPLE.1    PAGE 1 LINE 1 COL 01

       FIND? Example OPTIONS? (? FOR INFO)

***NOT FOUND: "Example" ***  Press ESCAPE Key ◄───Press ESCAPE
```

Note that the find command begins its search from the present location of the cursor. If you want your entire file searched, you must move the cursor to the beginning of the file before issuing the ^QF command.

Return the cursor to the beginning of the file. This time we will search for a word that occurs several times in the file. Type ^QF and, in response to FIND?, type **student** and press RETURN; press RETURN once more in response to OPTIONS?

WordStar advances through the file looking for the word "student"; the cursor passes over "Student" in the salutation to the letter because of the capital "S", but stops in the first line at the word "students". It has found the string of characters you requested, and it makes no difference that there is an extra "s" at the end. To go on and find the next occurrence of the word "student," type ^L; again the cursor stops after the word. Each time the cursor stops, you may delete the word, add a word, or do whatever editing you wish, then type ^L to continue the search for the word.

Find and Replace (^QA)

<8.07>   Return to the beginning of the file. We will use the find command now
[5-4]   in conjunction with replace. Type **^QA** and, in response to FIND?, type
         Outside and press RETURN. WordStar now responds: REPLACE
         WITH?. Type **Inside**, press RETURN, and press RETURN again in response
         to OPTIONS?

```
^QA    A:EXAMPLE.1 PAGE 1 LINE 1 COL 01 ──────── Press RETURN
       FIND? Outside REPLACE WITH? Inside ◄───── Press RETURN
       OPTIONS? (? FOR INFO)
                                          ──────── Press RETURN
```

The cursor advances to the first occurrence of Outside. In the status line is the question REPLACE Y/N?. Type **Y** and Outside is replaced with Inside.

```
^QA    A:EXAMPLE.1 PAGE 1 LINE 1 COL 01      REPLACE (Y/N): Y

       FIND? Outside REPLACE WITH? Inside
```

Type ^L and the cursor advances to the next occurrence of Outside with the question repeated. You can move through a file of any length in this manner, replacing or not with the **Y** or **N** response to the question. Now let's consider all the options.

Options

<8.07>   These options apply to both the **^QF** find command and the **^QA**
[5-4]   find-and-replace command. More than one option can be selected at a time; just enter the letters one after another, with no punctuation, before pressing RETURN.

number   Does the FIND or REPLACE *n* times, where *n* is an integer. For example, if *n* is 4, FIND the fourth occurrence of the word you are looking for or REPLACE the next four occurrences of the word with your substitution. The NOT FOUND error occurs if the command cannot be performed *n* times; as many FINDs or REPLACEs as are possible will have been done.

G   Searches the entire file, stopping at each occurrence of the word you are looking for, asking you to respond with a **Y** or **N** if you wish that FIND replaced. If no occurrences are found, WordStar responds with ***NOT FOUND ***. If used with the find command, it stops at the last occurrence of the word you are seeking.

N   Replaces the word sought without asking. This is convenient to use with G if you are sure all FINDs should be replaced.

B   Searches backward from the cursor position.

U   Ignores the difference between upper- and lower-case letters. For example, CASE matches case or Case.

W   Finds whole words only. Therefore, ace will not match
           race. Since a word has a space before and after it, this
           command will not find a match that is the first or last
           word in a file.

For a time-saving application of the find-and-replace command
(**^QA**), consider the following. Suppose you are writing a letter or report
that repeats the same phrase or long word several times. Each time that
word or phrase should be entered in the document, enter instead a
single, uncommon character such as the ampersand (**&**). When you
have finished the document, enter the find-and-replace command,
^QA. In response to the question FIND?, enter **&**. In response to the
REPLACE WITH? question, enter your word or phrase, and in
response to OPTIONS? enter **BGN**. WordStar will then search
backward through the entire file, automatically replacing the & with
your answer to the REPLACE WITH? question.

A word of caution: If you use the find-and-replace command to
search for a name or phrase containing two or more words, word wrap
may have inserted an extra space between adjacent words, so that
combination of words would not be found. To avoid this, search for a
single word. If it is necessary to search for a double word, as in the third
example in the section below, when the search is finished, do a
backward search through the file for the word Jones to be sure none of
the desired replacements have been missed.

Examples

Here are some examples of using the find and find-and-replace
commands.

```
^QF
FIND? student OPTIONS (? FOR INFO) 3
        ↑                            ↑
   Press RETURN                 Press RETURN
```

This example shows how to find the third occurrence of the word "student" after the cursor.

```
^QF
FIND? student OPTIONS? (? FOR INFO)  BUW
```
           Press RETURN   *Press RETURN*

The option B causes the search to move backward from the position of the cursor, U causes the search to ignore the distinction between upper- and lower-case letters, and W causes the search to find complete words only. WordStar will find "Student," but not "students."

```
^QA
FIND? John Jones REPLACE WITH? Bill Smith
```
           Press RETURN   *Press RETURN*
```
OPTIONS? (? FOR INFO)  GN
```
                      Press RETURN

The option G searches from the beginning of the file for John Jones, and the option N replaces it with Bill Smith without asking.

```
^QA
FIND? his REPLACE WITH? her
```
          Press RETURN   *Press RETURN*
```
OPTIONS? (?FOR INFO)  GUW
```
                      Press RETURN

The option G searches the entire file from the beginning, asking at each FIND if you want to replace; U ignores the distinction between upper- and lower-case, and W looks for whole words only.

EXERCISES

1. Type in Example 12. Using the find-and-replace command replace each occurrence of John Philip Smith with Sara Lee Brown.

2. Find each occurrence of his and change to her if appropriate.

3. Delete all spacing for paragraph indent. To do this, search for five spaces—press the space bar five times—and replace with no spaces (just press RETURN). Remember, you will have to indicate when to eliminate the spaces, since five spaces occur in other parts of the document.

EXAMPLE 12

LAST WILL AND TESTAMENT

OF

JOHN PHILIP SMITH

I, JOHN PHILIP SMITH, presently residing in the City of
Walnut Creek, Contra Costa County, California, being of sound
and disposing mind and memory, and not acting under duress,
menace, or undue influence of any kind or person whatsoever, do
hereby make, publish and declare this to be my Last Will and
Testament in the following manner:

ARTICLE I

I hereby revoke any and all former and other Wills and
Codicils made at any time heretofore by me.

ARTICLE II

It is my intent hereby to dispose of all my property,
whether real or personal, tangible or intangible, community or
separate, wheresoever situated, that I have the right to dispose
of by Will, including all property in which I shall hereafter
acquire any interest, and further including any and all property
as to which I may hereafter acquire a power of appointment by
Will.

(continued)

ARTICLE III

I hereby declare that I am not married. I have no children. I have no former marriages or issue of such.

ARTICLE IV

I hereby give, devise, and bequeath one-half (1/2) of the residue of my estate, real, personal, or mixed, of whatever kind and wheresoever situated, equally to my parents, JOHN SMITH and ANGELA SMITH, of Lovely Lane, Martinez Ca. 94553. If one parent shall predecease me, then the surviving parent shall take all, and then to their issue by right of representation.

ARTICLE V

I give, devise and bequeath one-half (1/2) of the residue of my estate, real, personal, or mixed, of whatever kind and wheresoever situated to my very good friend, MARCY SIMMONS, and then to her issue by right of representation. If MARCY SIMMONS shall predecease me, this gift shall lapse.

ARTICLE VI

I direct that all my debts, including funeral expenses, expenses of last illness, administration expenses, and all inheritance, estate, and other death taxes, and payment of a family allowance, if needed, be paid by the Executrix out of the residue of my estate from the first moneys coming into her hands and available therefor, and shall not be charged or collected from any beneficiary of my probate estate.

(continued)

ARTICLE VII

I hereby nominate and request the court to appoint my friend, MARCY SIMMONS, as Executrix of this Will, to serve without bond.   Should MARCY SIMMONS serve as Executrix, I authorize her to sell, lease, convey, transfer, encumber, hypothecate, or otherwise deal with the whole or any portion of my estate, either by public or private sale, with or without notice, and without securing any prior order of the court therefor.

I further authorize my Executrix either to continue the operation of any business belonging to my estate for such time and in such manner as she may deem advisable, and for the best interests of my estate, or to sell or liquidate the business at such time and on such terms as she may deem advisable, and for the best interests of my estate. Any operation, sale or liquidation made in good faith shall be at the risk of my estate, without liability for any resulting losses against the Executrix.

ARTICLE VIII

If any beneficiary under this Will, in any manner, directly or indirectly, contests, objects or attacks this Will or any of its provisions, any share or interest in my estate given to that contesting or objecting beneficiary under this Will is revoked and shall be disposed of in the same manner as if that beneficiary had predeceased me without issue.

(continued)

ARTICLE IX

I have intentionally and purposely omitted and made no provision in this Will for any person not mentioned herein, whether an heir of mine or one claiming to be an heir of mine or not; and if any person, whether or not mentioned in this Will should object, contest or attack this Will or any provision hereof, I give to such person, or to each of such persons, if more than one be so contesting or objecting, the sum of Ten Dollars ($10.00), and no more, in lieu of the provisions which I might have made for such person or persons so contesting, objecting or attacking this Will.

IN WITNESS WHEREOF, I subscribe my name to this, my Last Will and Testament, this _____ day of _____, 19___, at _____, Contra Costa County, California.

_____

JOHN PHILIP SMITH

(continued)

The foregoing instrument, consisting of four (4) pages and this fifth (5th) witness page, was, at this date, by the said JOHN PHILIP SMITH signed and published as and declared to be his Last Will and Testament in the presence of us, who, at his request, and in his presence, and in the presence of each other, have signed our names as witnesses hereto.

_____residing at_____

_____

_____residing at_____

_____

Working with Long Lines

[4-15]   All the work you have done up to now has had less than 80 characters per line; this is sufficient for most office work. Occasionally, however, you may be called on to work with documents that have more than 80 characters per line. Before you plan these documents, make sure you can print lines longer than 80 characters on your printer. You may be able to use .CW to print more characters per line (Lesson 9). You may also be able to print longer lines by using condensed print in your printer (Lesson 6).

WordStar allows you to set your right margin at any value up to column 32,000; however, it is not recommended that it be set greater than 240, since not all WordStar commands work efficiently beyond this value. For now, open a file and change the ruler line so that the right margin is at 132. If you have WordStar version 1.x or 2.x, you'll see that the ruler line is split on the screen so that the last part of the line is positioned under the first part of the line. Long lines of text will be displayed the same way, which means that one full line of text (132 characters) will appear as two lines on the screen. A flag character, "+", will appear in column 80 to indicate any line which, because of the right margin, must continue on a second line on your screen.

One of the major new features of WordStar 3.0 is the ability to scroll left and right for text lines wider than your screen (usually 80 characters). The right side of a line will extend off the screen until you have moved the cursor within that part of the line, rather than split the line on the screen. The screen will scroll left or right to display a "window" of text within the column area in which you are working.

When entering a program of this type, do some preliminary planning to determine correct placement of tabs, paper length, and so forth; then print the file after two or three lines have been entered to be sure it is printing out the way you want it to.

Now go on to the exercises for more hands-on instruction.

EXERCISES

1. Set up your ruler line with appropriate regular and decimal tabs to enter Example 13A. Move the cursor to the various tab positions to become used to split lines, or if you have WordStar 3.x, to become accustomed to time delay and changing screen when side scrolling. Example 13B shows sample screen display first for version 1.x and 2.x users, and then for version 3.x users.

2. Look at Examples 13C and 13D. Example 13D was printed out with WordStar and shows the final form of what was entered as Example 13C. Some printers do not support the **.CW** and **.LH** commands, and therefore will not be able to print this report as illustrated.

   Enter the chart illustrated in Example 13C.

   Before you begin entering the information, let's consider the restrictions imposed when this example was first assigned. The final version was to be printed on 8 1/2 × 11 paper. With the reducing copier available, the version from WordStar could be 11 inches wide. Using a 12-pitch type and the **.CW 10** command, 128 columns could be used for text, with some space left over for a margin on each side.

   First determine the proper tab settings. We need eight columns, one for teacher names and seven for class periods. With the proper ruler line and tabs set, enter the headings and the first two names, along with the lines that separate the names. In order for the complete list to be printed on a single sheet of paper, the dotted lines separating the teachers had to have the spacing changed with the **.LH** command. Enter these **.LH** commands now and notice that they have to be changed again to get the proper spacing between the first and last names of the teachers. When you have completed names and commands for the first two teachers, save and print the file.

EXAMPLE 13A

MARTINEZ UNIFIED SCHOOL DISTRICT

Purchasing Order
Report 2

P.O.#	VENDOR	PURPOSE	LOCATION	AMOUNT
32857	Radio Shack	Equipment	ROP	4,635.54
32858	Computer Center	Equipment	ROP	2,287.75
32861	ACE	Repairs	Maintenance	197.00
32862	National Motor Exchange	Parts	Transportation Dept.	49.26
32865	Scott Foresman	Books	Curriculum	14.79

```
L------------------|------------------------------!----------------------!------+
------------------------------#------------------------------R

                                              MARTINEZ UNIFIED SCHOOL DISTR+
ICT                              Purchasing Order                           <
                                                                            +
                                 Report 2                                   <
                                                                            <
P.O.#              VENDOR                       PURPOSE            LOCATIO+
N                      AMOUNT                                              <
------------------------------------------------------------------------+
------------------------------------------------------------                <
                                                                            <
                                                                            <
32857              Radio Shack                  Equipment         ROP     +
                       4,635.54                                             <
                                                                            <
32858              Computer Center              Equipment         ROP     +
                       2,287.75                                             <
                                                                            <
32861              ACE                          Repairs           Mainten+
ance                   197.00                                             <
                                                                            <
32862              National Motor               Parts             Transpo+
rtation                49.26                                               <
                       Exchange                                   Dept.<
                                                                            <
32865              Scott Foresman               Books             Curricu+
lum                    14.79                                               <
                                                                            <
```

```
L------------------|------------------------------!----------------------!------  <
                                                                            <
                                                                            <
                                              MARTINEZ UNIFIED SCHOOL DISTR <
                                                                            <
P.O.#              VENDOR                       PURPOSE            LOCATIO <
--------------------------------------------------------------------------  <
                                                                            <
                                                                            <
32857              Radio Shack                  Equipment         ROP       <
                                                                            <
32858              Computer Center              Equipment         ROP       <
                                                                            <
32861              ACE                          Repairs           Mainten <
                                                                            <
32862              National Motor               Parts             Transpo <
                       Exchange                                   Dept.   <
                                                                            <
32865              Scott Foresman               Books             Curricu <
                                                                            <
```

EXAMPLE 13C

STRANDS HIGH SCHOOL
CLASS SCHEDULE 1980-81

Teachers	Period 1 8:00-8:50	Period 2 8:55-9:45	Period 3 9:50-10:40	Period 4 11:02-11:52	Period 5 11:57-12:47	Period 6 1:22-2:12	Period 7
Janice Allen	Prep	B-4 Steno II / Short. Trans.	B-4 / Int. Typing	B-2 / Ofc. Sk.	B-4 / Steno I	B-4 / Int. Typing	
Roger Armstrong	H-1 / Draft. I	H-1 Draft.I,II / Adv. Draft.	H-1 Draft.I,II / Adv. Draft.	M-5 / Mod. Mat.	Prep	H-1 Draft.I,II / Adv. Draft.	
Margeret *Baker	G-2 / P.E.	G-2 / P.E.	G-2 / P.E.	G-2 / P.E.	C-2 / P.E.	Prep	
Lewis Bentley	A-24 / Chemistry	Prep	A-24 / Chemistry	A-24 / Algebra I	A-24 / Intro Alg. B	A-24 / Intro Alg. B	
Greg Carson	A-1 / Am. Pol. Pr.	G-1 / P.E.	G-1 / P.E.	Prep	G-1 / P.E.	G-1 / P.E.	
Joseph Clyne	C-1 / Gen. Math	C-1 / Intro Alg. A	C-1 / Tech Math	C-1 / Prep	C-1 / Algebra I	C-1 / Algebra I	
Angelica Fuente	Prep	T-3 / Com. Ideas	C-24 / Arith.	C-24 / Math Prep	C-24 / Remedial Math	C-24 / Anthro	
Carlos Duarte	A-20 / Soc. Stud.	A-20 / Reading	A-20 / Math	A-20 / Science	A-20 / Tutoring	A-20 / Prep	
Jaime Hernandez	H-22 / English Ix	H-22 / Com. Inag.	H-22 / English IIIx	H-22 / English Ix	H-22 / English IIIx	English IIIx	
Paul lakewood	A-21 / Tutoring Eng.	A-21 / Corr. Read. B	A-21 / Corr. Read. C	A-21 / U.S. Skills	A-21 / Corr. Read. D	Prep	

EXAMPLE 13D

STRANDS HIGH SCHOOL
CLASS SCHEDULE 1980-81

Teachers	Period 1 8:00-8:50	Period 2 8:55-9:45	Period 3 9:50-10:40	Period 4 11:02-11:52	Period 5 11:57-12:47	Period 6 1:22-2:12	Period 7
Janice Allen	Prep	B-4 Steno II / Short. Trans. H-1	B-4 Int. Typing / H-1 Draft.I,II/	B-2 Ofc. Sk. M-5	B-4 Steno I	B-4 Int. Typing / H-1 Draft.I,II/	
Roger Armstrong	Draft. I G-2	Adv. Draft. G-2	Adv. Draft G-2	Mod. Mat. G-2	Prep G-2	Adv. Draft. G-2	
Margaret Baker	P.E. A-24	P.E.	P.E. A-24	P.E. A-24	P.E. A-24	Prep A-24	
Lewis Bentley	Chemistry A-1	Prep G-1	Chemistry G-1	Algebra I G-1	Intro Alg. B G-1	Intro Alg. B G-1	
Greg Carson	Am. Pol. Pr. C-1	P.E. C-1	P.E. C-1	Prep C-1	P.E. C-1	P.E. C-1	
Joseph Clyne	Gen. Math A-20	Intro Alg. A A-20	Tech Math A-20	Prep A-20	Algebra I A-20	Algebra I	
Carlos Duarte	Soc. Stud. T-3	Reading T-3	Math C-24	Science C-24	Tutoring C-24	Prep C-24	
Angelica Fuente	Prep H-22	Com. Ideas H-22	Arith. H-22	Math Prep H-22	Remedial Math H-22	Anthro.	
Jaime Hernandez	English Ix A-21	Com. Imag. A-21	English IIIx A-21	English Ix A-21	English IIIx A-21	Prep	
Paul Lakewood	Tutoring Eng.	Corr. Read. B	Corr. Read. C	U.S. Skills	Corr. Read. D	Prep	

Miscellaneous Commands Menus

You're likely to find a few other commands, presented here, useful when entering or editing most files.

Besides the no-file menu, there are five additional menus you have access to while working with a WordStar file. After you've entered the menu prefix, the options for commands are displayed on the screen. When you have selected the option, the command will be entered in your file, and the screen display will return to your text.

Repeat (^QQ)

<8.12>
[6-10]
This is used to repeat a command at a controlled rate. For instance, if you wish to scroll through a file from beginning to end in order to proofread the file, place the cursor at the beginning of the file and type

$^\wedge$**QQZ**. The text will advance one line at a time onto the screen. The speed can be increased or decreased by pressing the numbers **1** through **9**; 1 is the fastest, 9 is the slowest, and 3 is the default value. Load in one of your examples and try it. You can also display successive screens, either forward or backward, by typing $^\wedge$**QQC** or $^\wedge$**QQR.**

Interrupt ($^\wedge$U)

<8.12>   This command, like the repeat process discussed previously, will
[6-10]   interrupt any command in progress. It can also be used when WordStar asks questions like FILE NAME? or FIND?. $^\wedge$U displays ***INTERRUPTED*** (unless nothing was interrupted) and requires you to press the ESCAPE key to continue editing.

Help Level ($^\wedge$JH)

<8.12>   This command allows you to select the amount of information displayed
[2-8]   on the screen. There are four selections, numbered 0-3; 3 displays the most information, 0 the least. With help level 0, only the status line and the ruler line are displayed; this allows more room for text, and the command sheet can be used for help.

Help Menu ($^\wedge$J)

[2-8]   Allows you to set the help level and to get on-screen instructions for many WordStar commands.

H	Set Help Level	M	Margin and Tabs
F	Flags in Right Column	S	Status Line
I	Command Index	R	Ruler Line
B	Paragraph Reform	V	Moving Text
D	Dot Command	P	Place Marker

Block Menu ($^\wedge$K)

[2-6]   Displays commands for saving files, block operations, and file and disk operations.

End Edit/Save
D Done Edit
X Done, Exit
S Save, Reedit
Q Abandon Edit

Mark Block
B Block Start
K Block End
H Hide/Display

Additional Files and Printing
R Read File
W Write Block
J Delete File

O Copy File
E Rename File
P Print File

Disk and Directory
L Change Logged Disk
F File Directory

Place Markers
0—9 Set place markers 0—9

On Screen Menu (^O)

[2-7] Displays commands for setting margins, tabs, and toggles.

S Line Spacing
L Left Margin
R Right Margin
I Tab Stop
N Clear Tab
G Paragraph Tab
C Center Text on Line
X Margin Release

W Word Wrap
J Justification
V Variable Tabs
H Hyphen Help
F Ruler File from Line
E Soft Hyphen
D Print Display
P Page Break
T Ruler Display

Print Menu (^P)

[2-7] Displays commands for special print effects.

V Subscript
S Underscore
A Alternate Pitch
O Non-break Space
C Printer Pause
Q, W, E, R User Printer Controls

T Superscript
B Boldface
N Standard Pitch
F Phantom Space
H Overprint

Quick Menu (^Q)

[2-5]   Displays commands for cursor movements, delete, and find.

Cursor

S	Left Screen	R	Beginning File
E	Top Screen	C	End File
X	Bottom Screen	0—9	To Marker
D	Right Screen	B, K, V, P	To Marker

Scroll   **Find, Replace**

Z	Continuous Up	F	Find a String
W	Continuous Down	A	Find and Substitute

Delete to End Line   **Repeat Next Command**

DEL	Left	Q	Until Key Pressed
Y	Right		

EXERCISES

1. Type in Example 14. Return to the beginning of the file and scroll through the file with the use of the repeat command. Try various speeds.

2. Use the interrupt command to stop the scrolling used above.

3. Display the various help levels discussed in this lesson.

EXAMPLE 14

SUGGESTIONS FOR COMPUTER CONFIGURATION AND USE IN M.U.S.D.

CLASSROOM I	Formal Programming Class 6 Stations, Printer (High Quality) Dual Disk Word Processing
CLASSROOM II	Formal Programming, CAI 6 Stations Printer (High Speed) Dual Disk Open for Individual Teachers
ADMINISTRATION	Two Stations: Printer Dual Disk - Hard Disk Word Processing
MOBIL UNIT	4 Stations to be used in various class- rooms and schools for short periods

USES:

1. TEACH:
    a. Basic Programming   - All Students
    b. Assembly Language   - MGM
    c. Word Processing   - Business Students
    d. Accounting(Bookkeeping) - Business Students
    e. Computer "Literacy"   - Bus. & Gen. Students
    f. Special Projects   - e.g., Plotter
    g. Journalism   - English Students

2. Computer Assisted Instruction (CAI)
    Useful in all areas - particularly for remedial work.

3. ADMINISTRATION:
    a. Attendance (H.S.)*   f. Physical Performance Test*
    b. Attendance & State Reports g. WASC*
       (elem.)*   h. District Handbook
    c. Scholarships*   i. District Directory
    d. Voc. Ed. (records)*   j. Reports
    e. OWE (records)*   k. Recordkeeping (misc.)

While building towards the desired computer facilities in the
school district, careful planning should be maintained to ensure
maximum compatibility of software between systems.

*Projects completed or in progress.

MailMerge— Form Letters With Data File

MailMerge is a supplement to WordStar and operates only in conjunction with it. MailMerge allows you to generate form letters with names, addresses, or other information automatically inserted in the format you wish. The information may come from a data file, or it may be entered from the keyboard at the appropriate time. We'll illustrate the use of MailMerge by developing an example.

There are a few symbols and dot commands used only with MailMerge which will be introduced in this lesson. They are

Command	Function
.DF	Data File name
.RV	Read Variable
&	Insertion of variable data
/O	Omit line with no data

Data File

[9-2] Begin by creating a data file. All of the files we have created so far with WordStar have been document files. Load WordStar and press **N** to select a non-document file. Name the file NAMES3.MRG and press RETURN.

The status line is different from that for a document file. You are presented with this status line (if your logged disk drive is B):

B: NAMES3.MRG FC=1 FL=1 Col 01

The disk drive and filename are shown in the same manner as for a document file. "FC" stands for *file character*; the number following will change to indicate the number of characters from the beginning of the file to the position of the cursor. "FL" stands for *file line* and indicates the number of lines from the beginning of the file to the line the cursor is on.

The non-document file begins with word wrap OFF. This is necessary so that you do not have any unintentional spaces or carriage returns entered into the file. Starting on line 1, column 1, enter the data from Example 15A just as it appears. Be sure to use exactly the same punctuation and spacing, and end each line by pressing RETURN.

Let's take a look at this data file. Each of the lines contains the same information or at least a place for that information.

Title:	Mr.
First name:	Henry
Last name:	Rath
Number and street:	123 Sack Street
Apartment number:	Apt. 6
City, State, ZIP:	Concord, CA 94520
Telephone number:	(415) 229-6251
Profession:	Legal

Each item of information in the data file is separated by a comma, and if an individual item contains a comma (such as city, state, ZIP), the entire item must be enclosed in quotes. Also notice that in the first line of the data file an apartment number is included for Henry Rath. On the next two lines an apartment number is not required, but you must still enter a comma (with no space in between) to maintain the position of all the data items.

Each of the lines in this data file is called a *record*. When creating your own data files, if your records are longer than will fit on the screen, you may place them on two lines for easier viewing. To do this, end an item with a RETURN instead of a comma (not both). Never press RETURN in the middle of an item. Here's an example: After the entry "Mr." you can press the RETURN key, but you cannot press RETURN in the middle of "Walnut Creek, CA." Also, do not place any dot commands in a data file, unless, of course, they are items in a record. Inspect the file you just typed in to be sure all the commas and quotes are in the proper places. Save the file in the normal manner with ^**KD**.

Form Letter

[9-3]   Type in Example 15B as a document file with the name POLIT1.MM. With generation of form letters, there are two areas to consider a little differently than with single-print documents. First, page numbering. Since it is assumed you are going to print the text of your file more than once, either **.OP** or **.PN** can be used to control page numbering. **.OP** omits page numbers altogether, which is appropriate for this single page letter. If your document were more than one page long and you wanted page numbers printed starting with page 1, each time the file is printed, you would enter **.PN 1**. As with any document file, this command should be entered at the beginning of the file, before any text has been entered.

    Second, page breaks. Be sure the **.PA** command is included at the end of your file so the printing of each subsequent letter will begin on a new page.

Data File Name (.DF)

[9-8]   Use **.DF** to tell MailMerge the name of the data file to get data from—in this case, the name of the data file you typed in previously (NAMES3.MRG). Notice also that when you type in this dot command, the letter "M" appears in the flag column. All MailMerge dot commands will cause an "M" to appear in the flag column.

Read Variable (.RV)

[9-9]   You must assign variable names to each of the items contained in a record of your data file. These variable names must be listed in the exact same order as that in which you entered the data in the data file records. Type **.RV**, a space, and then each variable name separated by commas. Avoid using commas, spaces, or other punctuation as part of the variable name. Variable names may contain up to 40 characters (letters and numbers).

Insertion Point (&)

[9-4]   A pair of ampersands (**&&**) is used to indicate where data from the data file should be entered into a printed document. Enclosed within each pair of ampersands is one of the variable names from the **.RV** command line.

     Variable names correspond to data in each record of the data file. When a document is printed, MailMerge inserts corresponding data in place of the variable name in the document file. You don't have to print each variable in the text of your document (but you *must* have a variable name entered in the **.RV** statement to correspond to each element of data in the data file being used). This allows you to use the same data file with different documents.

     When the first letter is printed, the items from the first record of the data file will be substituted for their corresponding variables. With the printing of the second, the items from the second record will be substituted, and so on. The number of records in a data file has no limit except for disk space.

Omitting Blank Lines (/O)

[10-10]   The insertion command for variable APT (apartment) contains the characters **/O**. This indicates to MailMerge that if there is no data for this item, as is the case for the second and third records, not to leave a blank line. **/O** must appear within the **&&** insertion characters for that variable.

Printing a MailMerge File

[9-9]   In order to print this file with MailMerge, be sure that the data file POLIT1.MM is on the same disk as your document file, or that a drive indentifier precedes the data file filename in the **.DF** command if the data file is in a different drive (for example, .DF C:NAMES3.MRG).

From the no-file menu, press **M**. You are presented with the question

NAME OF FILE TO MERGE-PRINT?

Enter the file name POLIT1.MM and press RETURN. You are now presented with the same series of questions as when printing a document file from WordStar, plus the additional question NUMBER OF COPIES (RETURN for 1)? MailMerge will print more than one copy of each letter if you request it to do so. Give your desired response for each question. MailMerge will print the form letter for each person in your data file. (If you requested multiple copies, it will print that number of copies of each letter.) A sample printed letter appears in Example 15C.

EXERCISES

1. Add the appropriate data for three more people to the NAMES3.MRG file. From the no-file menu, rename the file to NAMES6.MRG.

2. Using the political contributions letter, merge-print the file using NAMES6.MRG to verify that all the data was entered correctly.

EXAMPLE 15A

```
Mr.,HENRY,RATH,123 SACK ST.,APT. 6,"CONCORD, CA  94520",(415) 229-6251,legal
Mr.,KAT,BALLEW,6880 WALNUT BLVD.,"WALNUT CREEK, CA  94598",(415) 698-3320,medical
Ms.,EFFIE,CARLSON,214 MIDHILL DR.,"MARTINEZ, CA  95443",(415) 228-3006, teaching
```

EXAMPLE 15B

```
.OP
.DF NAMES3.MRG
.RV TITLE,FNAME,LNAME,STREET,APT,CITY,PHONE,PROF



                DESERT SPRINGS COUNTY SUPERVISORS OFFICE
                    COUNTY BUILDING - SUITE 3001A
                        2105 WEST ACACIA BLVD.
                 DESERT SPRINGS, CALIFORNIA  94562
                          (707) 324-9109

                        July 9, 1982



&TITLE& &FNAME& &LNAME&
&STREET&
&APT/O&
&CITY&


Dear &TITLE& &LNAME&:

In my three terms serving as your County Supervisor, I hope my
honest support of the &PROF& profession has earned your trust and
your vote.  More than that &TITLE& &LNAME& I hope you can see
your way clear to the modest campaign contribution of $25.00 tax
deductible dollars.


Sincerely,



Jerome P. Hunnycutt
County Supervisor

JH:sb
.PA
```

DESERT SPRINGS COUNTY SUPERVISORS OFFICE
COUNTY BUILDING - SUITE 3001A
2105 WEST ACACIA BLVD.
DESERT SPRINGS, CALIFORNIA 94562
(707) 324-9109

July 9, 1982

Mr. KAT BALLEW
6880 WALNUT BLVD.
WALNUT CREEK, CA 94598

Dear Mr. BALLEW:

In my three terms serving as your County Supervisor, I hope my
honest support of the medical profession has earned your trust
and your vote. More than that Mr. BALLEW I hope you can see your
way clear to the modest campaign contribution of $25.00 tax
deductible dollars.

Sincerely,

Jerome P. Hunnycutt
County Supervisor

JH:sb

MailMerge—
Form Letters with
Keyboard Entry

In Lesson 15, the source of the data used for MailMerge was a data file. You can also enter variable data into form letters while they are being printed without setting that data up in a data file. We will introduce the following new dot commands in this lesson:

Command	Function
.AV	Ask for Variable
.CS	Clear Screen
.DM	Display Message
.RP	Repeat File Processing
.SV	Set Variable

Keyboard Data Entry

[10-1]   To enter data from the keyboard into a MailMerge document, you need to enter a series of commands. In effect, these commands tell MailMerge to take data from the keyboard rather than from the data file. (You can enter data from the keyboard, plus get data from a data file, in the same document.) Let's work with the POLIT1.MM file from Lesson 15.

Suppose you want to vary the contribution requested from $25 to some other value based on the person's profession, past contributions, or some other basis. At the beginning of the file, just after the **.RV** command, enter the following:

```
.CS
.DM Contribution request from: &LNAME&—profession: &PROF&
.AV "Amount of contribution?", AMOUNT
```

Let's look at each of these commands.

Ask for Variable (.AV)

[10-5]   With this command, you specify the variable to be entered from the keyboard. Similar to using a data file, when MailMerge reaches the **.AV** variable name, it will replace that variable name with actual data. The difference is that you must enter that data from the keyboard, rather than MailMerge getting it from the data file.

In the **.AV** line we entered, the variable name specified is AMOUNT. This variable name must also be entered in the document file, with two surrounding **&** characters used to identify it as an insertion variable. In the text of the letter, replace **25** in ($25.00) with **&AMOUNT&**.

When you print this file, MailMerge will know that AMOUNT is a variable, and that it should *ask* for that data. It "asks" by printing a message on the screen, prompting you to enter the data. The message it prints is the message you typed in the **.AV** command, in this case, "Amount of contribution?". This message *must* be enclosed in quotation marks, and a comma separates it from the variable name.

When you enter this variable data, you are limited to the number of characters that will take you to the end of the line on your screen.

Note: Depending on the characteristics of your printer, the point in your file where the printer is stopped may not appear to coincide with the data you are entering. Enter data according to the prompt messages, and MailMerge will print the document as desired. If you have more than one variable to "ask" for in a letter, each variable should be entered in a separate **.AV** command line. For example, if you enter the commands

    .AV NAME
    .AV TITLE

when you merge-print, you will enter data on the screen as follows (the program prompts you with the variable name):

    NAME? **Jennifer** ↑*Press* RETURN
    TITLE? **Teacher** ↑*Press* RETURN

Clear Screen (.CS)

[11-3]   Many times it is appropriate to use MailMerge's clear screen command in conjunction with the **.AV** command. If **.CS** is placed in your file ahead of **.AV**, then each time MailMerge asks for data to be entered, the request will be made on a clear screen. This is particularly useful when there are several keyboard entries for each letter.

    You have the option of entering a message after the **.CS** command, such as **.CS Enter data as requested**.

Display Message (.DM)

[11-2]   The command **.DM** allows you to display a message on the screen. This message may include variable names from the **.RV** command line (as in the entry you made to file POLIT1.MM, where the variable data was displayed in the screen message). If a **.DM** message is used as a prompt for **.AV** keyboard entry, be sure it's entered *after* the **.CS** command.

Repeat (.RP)

[11-11]   The repeat command is useful when processing files which use only variable keyboard data entry and do not access a data file. The **.DF**

command causes a file to be processed as many times as there are records in a data file. Without this data file command, use **.RP** to specify how many times to process the file. Enter a space and the desired number after the command (for example, **.RP 8**). Enter this command with the other dot commands at the beginning of your file.

Set Variable (.SV)

[11-2]   Before we leave this lesson, let's add one additional dot command to the file.

In the current example we change the name and address for each letter. But there are situations where either a variable will be the same for several letters or the same variable might change several times in the same letter.

As an example of the first case, suppose you are sending several of the "request for contributions" letters out each day. The date on the letter therefore becomes a variable. To enter it each day, you can use the **.SV** command. With the other dot commands at the beginning of your file, add **.SV DATE, July 22, 1982**. This specifies DATE as a variable name, and the text following the comma is the actual data for that variable (the second comma is acceptable here). In place of the date in your letter, identify the insertion variable with **&DATE&**. Your file letterhead should now look like the following:

DESERT SPRINGS COUNTY SUPERVISORS OFFICE
COUNTY BUILDING - SUITE 3001A
2105 WEST ACACIA BLVD.
DESERT SPRINGS, CALIFORNIA 94562
(707) 324-9109
&DATE&

For each day that you send out a series of these letters, the date is entered only once in the **.SV** command line.

For the second case we need a longer example. Take a look at Example 12 from Lesson 12. In a will, the same names normally occur several times. In place of the actual names, the variables NAME1, NAME2, and so forth, can be substituted. The **.SV** command is used at the beginning of the file to identify the actual name that should replace each variable in the text. You can then type in the names once and they will be changed throughout the document. Each variable must be entered with a separate **.SV** command.

   Note: Any time something is centered, as is the name in the will heading, it is easier to type in the complete name rather than **&NAME1&** to ensure proper centering.

EXERCISES

1. Print the political contributions letter as set up in this lesson, entering the contribution amount from the keyboard, and setting the date with the .SV dot command. *Hint:* The dot commands and a keyboard entry sequence are shown in Example 16A.

2. Print the political contributions letter from Lesson 15, but this time entering names and addresses from the keyboard instead of from a data file.

3. Print the will from Lesson 12, entering the name of the deceased and friend only once. Example 16B shows the dot commands and three sections of the document file. Note that you must use the MailMerge print function to print this document, rather than the normal WordStar print function.

```
.OP
.DF NAMES3.MRG
.RV TITLE,FNAME,LNAME,STREET,APT,CITY,PHONE,PROF
.SV DATE, July 9, 1982
.CS
.DM Contribution request for: &LNAME& ,profession - &PROF&
.AV "Amount of contribution ?",AMOUNT
```

merge-printing B:POLIT1.MM   editing no file

P= STOP PRINT

Contribution request for: RATH ,profession - legal
Amount of contribution ?50
↑*Press* RETURN

EXAMPLE 16B

```
.PN 1
.SV NAME1, JOHN PHILIP SMITH
.SV NAME2, MARCY SIMMONS
```

LAST WILL AND TESTAMENT

OF

JOHN PHILIP SMITH

I, &NAME1&, presently residing in the City of Walnut Creek, Contra Costa County, California, being of sound and disposing mind and memory, and not acting under duress, menace, or undue influence of any kind or person whatsoever, do hereby make, publish and declare this to be my Last Will and Testament in the following manner:

ARTICLE V

I give, devise and bequeath one-half (1/2) of the residue of my estate, real, personal, or mixed, of whatever kind and wheresoever situated to my very good friend, &NAME2&, and then to her issue by right of representation. If &NAME2& shall predecease me, this gift shall lapse.

ARTICLE VII

I hereby nominate and request the court to appoint my friend, &NAME2&, as Executrix of this Will, to serve without bond. Should &NAME2& serve as Executrix, I authorize her to sell, lease, convey, transfer, encumber, hypothecate, or otherwise deal with the whole or any portion of my estate, either by public or private sale, with or without notice, and without securing any prior order of the court therefor.

MailMerge—
Special Printing

LESSON 17

Sometimes you'll create a file primarily to direct printing from a data file, a document file, or both. This lesson introduces the following final MailMerge dot commands:

Command	Function
.FI	File Insert
.PF	Print Formatting
.RM	Right Margin
.LM	Left Margin
.OJ	Output Justification
.IJ	Input Justification

Printing Data Files

Enter the information from Example 17A into a data file with the name NAMES8.MRG (remember, this should be a non-document file). Since it is difficult to read this type of file (to proofread it, for example) we'll create a command file to print it in a more readable format.

133

Open a document file with the name CLIENT.FIL and enter the following:

```
.DF NAMES8.MRG
.RV NAME,STREET,CITY,ZIP,PHONE,PROF
.CP 8
        (blank line)
        (blank line)
        &NAME&
        &STREET&
        &CITY&
        &ZIP&
        &PHONE&
        &PROF&
```

We can omit the **.PN** or **.OP** at the beginning of this file since we will not do any repeat printing of the same information. **.CP 8** is used to avoid printing a portion of the same person's data on different pages. Do not leave any blank lines below "&PROF&".

Save the file. From the no-file menu press **M**, and merge-print the file CLIENT.FIL to read the text in your data file.

Addressing Envelopes

[10-8]   As a second example we will write a file to direct the addressing of envelopes. Open a document file with the name ENVELOPE.MM and enter the following:

```
.PL 33
.PO 5
JACK SMITH
150 MAIN ST
MARTINEZ, CA 94553
.PO 40
.DF NAMES8.MRG.
.RV NAME,STREET,CITY,ZIP,PHONE,PROF
(blank line)
&NAME&
&STREET&
&CITY&
^P^C (this entry will appear as ^C on your screen)
.PA
```

The **.PL** command sets the length for the envelopes. Choose the value so that the envelopes are released from the printer after each envelope is printed. (**.PL 30** is equal to 5 inches.)

.PO 5 changes the default page offset from 8/10 to 5/10 of an inch for correct placement of the return address. If you use envelopes with a preprinted return address, this command would be omitted.

.PO 40 is used to place the address on the correct area of the envelope. You may also place **&NAME&**, **&STREET&**, and **&CITY&** in the proper column of your file, but the page offset command allows you to change easily to envelopes of different sizes.

^P^C, which will appear as **^C** on your screen, causes the printer to pause after each envelope is printed. This gives you time to insert the next envelope.

Try printing an envelope. Make adjustments to the print commands as needed to correctly align the addressing on your envelopes.

File Insert (.FI)

[11-4]   The file insert command allows one file to print text from another file as if it were part of the first file. You can create a file just to control the printing of various files, or insert files to print within your text document.

Two examples of these special print files are shown below. Each example shows how the file will appear on the screen. Pay particular attention to the symbols in the flag column. Notice that after each file insert command, a RETURN is entered. A final RETURN should be entered after the last **.FI** command.

This first example is the simplest form of a file containing the file insert command. The three files are printed out continuously with only a single space between the files.

```
.FI  SECTION.1                                      <
                                                    M
.FI  SECTION.2                                      <
                                                    M
.FI  SECTION.3                                      <
                                                    M
                                                    <
```

For the second example, open a document file and call it PRINTDOC.123. Enter the text shown in the following example. Notice that this file has two additional features.

```
.FI  SECTION.1                                                       <
.PA                                                                  M
----------------------------------------------------------------------P
.FI  B:SECTION.2                                                     M
.PA                                                                  <
----------------------------------------------------------------------P
.FI  B:SECTION.3 CHANGE                                             M
                                                                     <
```

First, if the **.PA** is placed between the file insert commands, each section that is printed will begin on a new page. Second, if the files you are printing reside on more than one disk, you may add the change command. Adding **CHANGE** after SECTION.3 allows you to change the disks in drive B before SECTION.3 is printed. The printer will stop after SECTION.2 is printed, and the following message will be displayed:

> INSERT DISKETTE WITH FILE B: SECTION.3 THEN
>   PRESS RETURN:

When MailMerge is ready for you to reinsert the disk with the special print command file, you will be presented with the message

> INSERT DISKETTE WITH FILE B:PRINTDOC.123, THEN
>   PRESS RETURN:

The final section will then be printed.

Letters and Envelopes

[10-10] In this application of the file insert command, we will print a form letter and address the envelopes. The printer will pause allowing for the insertion of letterhead and envelopes. To accomplish this, we will need four files: (1) a file to direct printing, (2) a form letter file, (3) an

envelope printing file, and (4) a data file. Assemble the following four files on one disk.

1. Open a document file with the name LETENV.MM and enter the following:

   .FI B:POLIT1.MM
   (line space)
   .FI B:ENVELOP2.MM

   Don't forget to press RETURN after the second .FI command.
   Save the file. It will direct the printing of the letters and envelopes.

2. Edit the file POLIT1.MM so the dot commands appear as follows:

   .OP
   .DF NAMES6.MRG
   .RV TITLE,FNAME,LNAME,STREET,APT,CITY,PHONE,PROF
   .CS
   .DM INSERT LETTERHEAD
   ^P^C (Remember, only ^C appears on the screen)

   Save the file. This creates our sample form letter file.

3. Open a file with the name ENVELOP2.MM and enter the following:

   .OP
   .PO 40
   .DF NAMES6.MRG
   .RV TITLE,FNAME,LNAME,STREET,APT,CITY,PHONE,PROF
   .CS
   .DM INSERT ENVELOPE
   ^P^C
   (line space)
   &TITLE& &FNAME& &LNAME&
   &STREET&
   &APT/O&
   &CITY&

   Save the file. This will print an envelope for each form letter.

4. The data file NAMES6.MRG is unchanged from Lesson 16.

With the four files on the same disk, place the disk in drive B. Press **M** from the no-file menu and merge-print file LETENV.MM. Appropriate prompts will be displayed when you are to insert letterhead or envelopes, and when you should continue printing.

Mailing Labels

[10-8]   We will use the data file NAMES8.MRG with a print command file to print out mailing labels. Open a document file. Name it ML.MM. Enter Example 17B as far as the last **.RV** dot command.

   Before proceeding further, consider the portion of the example you have just entered. A model is shown at the top of the file for a nonprinting ruler line. You can adjust the tabs later to fit your mailing labels. The **.MT** and **.MB** commands set top and bottom margins to 0 since most mailing label forms are spaced evenly from one sheet to the next. **.DF** gives the name of the file containing the data you are going to use. The next three lines contain **.RV** commands. We need three since we are going to print the labels three across. If the labels were two across, we would need two **.RV** command lines, if they were four across, four, and so on.

   The variables in the first **.RV** line will hold the information from the first record of the data file, the second **.RV** variables from the second record, and the third **.RV** from the third record. This sequence will repeat itself with the **.RV** commands gathering information from successive groups of three records as it proceeds through the data file. Note that we did not have to distinguish the variables PHONE and PROF with numbers since these data are not being printed.

   Entering the variables at the appropriate place in our print command file is somewhat confusing because the variable insert commands don't appear on the screen the way the data will be printed. What does appear on the screen will look like Example 17B. In order to have the names appear on the same line when printed out, we need a carriage return character without a linefeed (a linefeed drops the printer down to the next line). In order to accomplish this with WordStar, you need to press ^P and then RETURN.

   With the cursor in column 1, on the line below the third **.RV** command enter **&NAME1&** ^P RETURN. The cursor will move down one line and to the left. Press the TAB key (or ^I) so the cursor moves to column 25. Enter **&NAME2&** ^P RETURN. Tab over twice to column 50, and enter **&NAMES&** RETURN (no ^P). Follow the same procedure to enter &STREET1& &STREET2& &STREET3&, &CITY1& &CITY2& &CITY3&, and &ZIP1& &ZIP2& &ZIP3&, pressing ^P after the first two and only RETURN after the last. Compare your screen with Example 17B; they should look the same.

Save the file, and from the no-file menu, press **M**. Merge-print ML.MM; this should print the mailing labels. The format of sample printed labels is shown in Example 17C.

When the file looks for the third set of data in the third line, there is no more data. The following message will appear on your screen:

***WARNING: Data exhausted. Null value(s) used

This message does not harm your program.

Print-Time Line Forming

[12-1]   Normally the print formatting of the MailMerge output is handled by the print controls in the files being processed, but the following additional commands are available for use and affect files when they are being printed with MailMerge.

[12-3]   **.PF** — Print Formatting (**.PF** ON/OFF/DIS). (DIS means discretionary.) Print formatting must be on (**.PF ON**) in order for any of the following commands to function.

[12-3]   **.RM** — Right Margin (.RM n/DIS). Sets right margin to the desired value. (Enter any number between 1 and 240 in place of the ''n.'')

[12-4]   **.LM** — Left Margin (.LM n/DIS). Sets the left margin to the desired value (which is any number between 1 and 240 that you enter in place of the ''n'').

[12-4]   **.OJ** — Output Justification (.OJ ON/OFF/DIS). To justify the right margin, enter **.OJ ON**. For a ragged right margin, enter **.OJ OFF**.

[12-5]   **.IJ** — Input Justification (.IJ ON/OFF/DIS). **.IJ ON** interprets the right margin of the material coming to MailMerge as right-justified, which can then be changed with the **.OJ OFF** command. **.IJ OFF** interprets the right margin of the material coming to MailMerge as ragged, which can then be changed with the **.OJ ON** command.

The default value for all of the print-time line forming commands is discretionary (DIS). This means that formatting will depend on other format and print commands.

EXERCISES

1. Change your file CLIENT.FIL so that the client information appears in two columns instead of one. Use the procedure presented in the mailing label example.

2. Create a command file to address envelopes, assuming they have a preprinted return address.

3. Create a command file to print out four of your existing files in succession. Use the change option in at least one **.FI** command.

4. Redo the mailing label example to the format of the mailing labels you use.

EXAMPLE 17A

```
HENRY RATH,123 SACK ST.,"WALNUT CREEK, CALIF.",94598,(415) 229-6251,legal
KAT BALLEW,6880 WALNUT BLVD.,"WALNUT CREEK, CALIF.",94598,(415) 698-3320,medical
EFFIE CARLSON,214 MIDHILL DR.,"MARTINEZ, CALIF.",95443,(415) 228-3006, teaching
RALPH KNIGHT,370 MAIN ST.,"PLEASANT HILL, CALIF.",94520,(415) 378-5567,teaching
CARL CARLSON,989 PEACH BLVD.,"CONCORD, CALIF.",94520,(415) 228-2459,medical
GEORGE GODFREY,1891 ALHAMBRA AVE.,"MARTINEZ, CALIF.",94553,(415) 372-6483,legal
DAVID PEREZ,4830 PRIMROSE LN.,"PLEASANT HILL, CALIF.",94520,(415) 698- 5620,teaching
STEVE QUINN,659 FRANKLIN RD.,"WALNUT CREEK, CALIF.",94598,(415) 229-6578,medical
```

EXAMPLE 17B

```
    ..                                                                        -
    ---------------------------!--------------------------!----------------------<
.MT Ø                                                                          <
.MB Ø                                                                          <
.OP                                                                            <
.DF NAMES8.MRG                                                                 M
.RV NAME1,STREET1,CITY1,ZIP1,PHONE,PROF                                        M
.RV NAME2,STREET2,CITY2,ZIP2,PHONE,PROF                                        M
.RV NAME3,STREET3,CITY3,ZIP3,PHONE,PROF                                        M
&NAME1&                                                                        -
                        &NAME2&                                                -
                                               &NAME3&                         <
&STREET1&                                                                      -
                        &STREET2&                                              -
                                               &STREET3&                       <
&CITY1&                                                                        -
                        &CITY2&                                                -
                                               &CITY3&                         <
&ZIP1&                                                                         -
                        &ZIP2&                                                 -
                                               &ZIP3&                          <
                                                                              <
                                                                              <
                                                                              <
                                                                              .
```

EXAMPLE 17C

```
HENRY RATH               KAT BALLEW               EFFIE CARLSON
123 SACK ST.             6880 WALNUT BLVD.        214 MIDHILL DR.
WALNUT CREEK, CALIF.     WALNUT CREEK, CALIF.     MARTINEZ, CALIF.
94598                    94598                    95443


RALPH KNIGHT             CARL CARLSON             GEORGE GODFREY
370 MAIN ST.             989 PEACH BLVD.          1891 ALHAMBRA AVE.
PLEASANT HILL, CALIF.    CONCORD, CALIF.          MARTINEZ, CALIF.
94520                    94520                    94553


DAVID PEREZ              STEVE QUINN
4830 PRIMROSE LN.        659 FRANKLIN RD.
PLEASANT HILL, CALIF.    WALNUT CREEK, CALIF.
94520                    94598
```

SpellStar

LESSON 18

Like MailMerge, SpellStar is a supplement to WordStar and can be used only in conjunction with WordStar. SpellStar's function is to perform a spelling check on a WordStar file. It does this by using a dictionary file. SpellStar comes with a dictionary of approximately 20,000 words, and you can add your own words in a supplemental dictionary.

The procedure you use with SpellStar will vary slightly depending on the capacity of your disk system. We'll go through a general procedure first, assuming ample disk space on two drives. Later, a variation for smaller disks will be discussed.

Operations

Place your WordStar disk in drive A. It should contain files WS.COM, WSMSGS.OVR, WSOVLY1.OVR, SPELSTAR.OVR, and SPELSTAR.DCT. In drive B place the disk containing the file you wish

145

to check for spelling errors. Enter WordStar, and from the no-file menu, press **S** to enter SpellStar. Your screen will display the message

NAME OF FILE TO CHECK/ADD TO DICTIONARY

Type **B:SPELL.EX1** and press RETURN. You will now be presented with the following operations menu:

```
    OPERATIONS

C - Check Spelling
M - Maintain Dictionary
X - Exit to WordStar no-file menu

Operation? __
```

[13-1]   The three menu options are as follows:

C — Check Spelling. When you check for spelling errors in a WordStar file, SpellStar compares the words in your file against those in the dictionary; if it does not find a match, it "flags" the words with the symbols ^@ in your file to indicate that a match was not found. Of course, this does not necessarily mean a spelling error. You can then proceed to edit the file with WordStar.

M — Maintain Dictionary. The dictionary maintenance portion of SpellStar allows you to add words to or delete words from your current dictionary, or to create a new one. For instance, if you work in a doctor's office, you may wish to create a dictionary of medical terms. Dictionaries of legal, medical, or similar terms may also be purchased and processed with the maintenance section to run with SpellStar. A list of customer names or vendors that your firm does business with is also a likely candidate for a supplemental dictionary.

X — Exit. Return to the WordStar no-file menu.

Spelling Check Controls

[13-2]   From the SpellStar operations menu, enter **C**. You will be presented
with the following menu:

```
              Spelling Check Operation

 Spelling Check Controls              Current Value

 D - Use another main dictionary=     A:SPELSTAR.DCT
 S - Add supplemental dictionary=
 F - Change file to be checked=       B: SPELL.EX1
 W - Change work drive=               A:

 <Return> - Start spelling check
    X - Exit to Operations Menu

 Control to change? __
```

Let's look at the options individually.

D — Use another main dictionary. The disk drive and the name of the
dictionary your file will be checked against are indicated under
CURRENT VALUE. In this case you are using drive A and
SPELSTAR.DCT, the dictionary supplied by MicroPro.

S — Add supplemental dictionary. The file name for this option is
currently blank. You have the choice here of leaving it blank or adding a
second dictionary to compare your file against. This second dictionary
could be one you create yourself or one that has been purchased.

F — Change file to be checked. The disk drive and the file name that
you told SpellStar to check are given under CURRENT VALUE. By
choosing this option you can select a new file to process.

W — Change work drive. The drive indicated here is the same as your
logged drive. There must be sufficient space on this drive for SpellStar
to create the temporary files it needs while checking words in your file
against the chosen dictionary. The work space needed is approximately
the same size as the file being checked.

RETURN — Start spelling check. When you are ready to start the spelling check, press RETURN.

X — Exit to operations menu. If for some reason you do not wish to proceed further, you may press **X** to retrace your path back to the operations menu.

Before we proceed further, let's consider how to change these current values.

Choose option **D**, **F**, or **S** if there is a supplemental directory. Then proceed to change the information listed under CURRENT VALUE using the following rules:

1. To change only the disk drive, enter the new value and a colon. For example, to change the main dictionary from drive A to drive B, type **B:** RETURN.

2. To change only the file name, type the new file name and RETURN. For example, to change SPELSTAR.DCT to LEGAL.DCT, type **LEGAL** RETURN.

3. To change only the extension, type a period and the new extension. For example, to change the extension .DCT to .SUP, type **.SUP** RETURN.

4. To change any two of the three possibilities, type them in order and press RETURN. For example, to change SPELSTAR.DCT to LEGAL.SUP, type **LEGAL.SUP** RETURN. To change the drive from A to B and the extension from .DCT to .SUP, type **B:.SUP** RETURN.

5. To change the work drive, just type the letter (no RETURN).

Check Spelling

Press RETURN from the previous menu to proceed with the spelling check. The status line and the following table now appear on the screen (without the numbers on the right):

```
[SpellStar - Spelling check Operations  [checking B:SPELL.EX1]

SpellStar is now checking your document for misspelled words.

     Number of words in document. . . . . . . : 422
     Number of different words. . . . . . . . : 261
     Number of words in main dictionary . . . : 21182
     Number of words in supplement. . . . . . :
     Number of dictionary words checked . . . : 21128
     Number of misspelled words . . . . . . . : 28
     Total number of misspellings . . . . . . :
```

[13-6]   SpellStar is now checking your document for misspelled words. As SpellStar processes your file, the numbers for each of the lines in the table are filled in, except for the last line, "total number of misspellings," which is filled in later.

Keep in mind that the line indicating the number of misspelled words really means the number of words in your file for which no match was found in the dictionary. This may mean the words were misspelled, or it could mean they are not in the dictionary and may or may not be spelled correctly.

Once SpellStar has completed the spelling check, you have the following options:

L — List misspelled words. This option lists the unmatched words in alphabetical order on the screen. If more than one screen of words is in the list, you may press the space bar for the next screen, press **C** for continuous listing, or press ^L to stop listing and return to the menu. (*Note*: You are presented with these options only when the list of misspelled words is longer than will fit in a single screen.)

F — Flag file. Press RETURN to flag the unmatched words in your file. This flagged file will be created on the same disk as your original file, unless you indicated otherwise when you started SpellStar. The name for the file with the flagged words will be the same as your original, but will have .@@@ as the extension. When the flagging is completed, you may correct the file or terminate SpellStar to perform some other task.

R — Restart. This returns you to the WordStar no-file menu.

Editing a Flagged File

Pressing RETURN to edit the flagged file returns you to WordStar and presents you with the following menu:

```
F - Fix Word          A - Add to dictionary
B - Bypass Word       S - Add to supplemental dictionary
I - Ignore Word
```

Your flagged file is on the screen with the cursor at the beginning of the first flagged word. You have WordStar's full editing capabilities, but first you must choose from one of the menu options. Let's look at these options individually.

F — Fix Word. If you decide the first flagged word needs "fixing," press ^F and change the word appropriately. When you are satisfied with the spelling of the word, press L, and the cursor will move quickly to the next flagged word. If you wish to move backward in your file to the previously flagged word, type ^QL. You may turn off these flags in your file by typing OD. Typing ^OD again will turn the flags back on. The purpose, of course, is to see how your file will appear in printed form.

B — Bypass Word. Pressing **B** bypasses the word so that the cursor will move on to the next flagged word. The current word remains flagged.

I — Ignore Word. Pressing **I** causes the cursor to move on to the next word and also removes the flag from the current word. (*Note*: When you press **I**, SpellStar remembers the words to ignore and will stop only briefly the next time it encounters one of these words, and then will automatically move to the next word. If you press **I** during this brief stop, it will ignore the following word. It has a limited capacity in this function and will retain in memory only the last 20 words it was told to ignore.)

A — Add to dictionary. If the cursor stops at a word you use frequently that is not in the main dictionary, press **A**. This will store the word in a special ADD file which you may use later to supplement your main dictionary. Of course, be certain the word is spelled correctly.

S — Add to supplemental dictionary. The function here is the same as pressing **A** except that the word will go into a supplemental dictionary.

When the SpellStar check is completed, you are at the end of your WordStar file. You will receive the message

PRESS THE ESCAPE KEY

This will return you to WordStar, with the cursor at the end of the file.

When you edit a file with SpellStar, you have two other options. You can start the edit and finish it at a later time, or you can postpone all the editing until later. Let's run through these two options now.

If you are working with a long file and would like to start editing now and finish the job later, you may interrupt the editing process by pressing ^U. Save the file with ^**KD**. When you are ready to continue making your corrections, enter WordStar and open the document file. The partially corrected file will have the same name as the file you ran the spelling check on, but with the extension .@@@ . Enter this name, and when the text appears on the screen, press ^**QL**. You will then be presented with the message

RETURN=search forward, B=search backward,
G=from start of file:

Move to the point in your file where the flagged words appear and make the corrections just as you did previously. When you have finished editing the flagged file and have the cursor at the end of the file, make one additional pass backward through the file to be sure you have not missed any flagged words. Do this by pressing ^**QL** and **B**. This causes the search to proceed backward through the file with the cursor stopping at any flagged words that you may have bypassed or missed in the first edit.

If you postponed all the editing, when you are ready to begin, enter

WordStar and edit the file with the .@@@ extension. When the editing is completed and you have saved the file, it will have the name of the original file, and the file with the errors will have the original name with the extension changed to .BAK.

Limited Disk Storage

If you are using 5 1/4-inch disks with limited storage, use the following procedure to work with SpellStar.

With a large file to check you'll need three disks. The first is your WordStar disk, and it should contain the files WS.COM, WSMSGS.OVR, WSOVLY1.OVR, and SPELSTAR.OVR. The second disk should contain SPELSTAR.DCT, and the third disk should have your file on it.

Place the WordStar disk in drive A and SPELSTAR.DCT in drive B. Proceed as outlined, loading WordStar and selecting **S** for SpellStar. From the SpellStar menu choose option **C** to check spelling; then replace the WordStar disk with the third disk. Proceed until you have flagged the file. Before you begin the edit, replace the third disk with the WordStar disk.

If the file you wish to check is small enough, you may be able to place it on the disk with the dictionary and work with just two disks. Remember, though, you need work space equal to the size of your file on the disk that contains your file.

Dictionary Maintenance

[13-11]   This section of SpellStar allows you to add or delete words from existing dictionaries or to create a new one. Select option **M** from the SpellStar operations menu, and you will be presented with the following menu:

```
        SpellStar - Dictionary Maintenance

    DICTIONARY MAINTENANCE CONTROLS              CURRENT VALUE

F - Change word file to use                   = A:FILENAME.XXX
D - Change dictionary to update               = A:SPELSTAR.DCT
U - Change name of new or update dictionary   = A:
W - Change work drive for sort                =      A:

    DICTIONARY MAINTENANCE OPTIONS

N - Create a new dictionary                   = NO
A - Add words                                 = NO
T - Delete words                              = NO
C - Combine add/delete                        = YES
S - Use "S" words from "ADD" file             = NO
L - List dictionary words                     = NO

<Return> - Start dictionary maintenance.
   X     - Exit to Operations menu

Control or option to change? __
```

Using the options here is very similar to what you did when working with the spelling check menu. Choosing the appropriate letter from the first column allows you to change the information in the CURRENT VALUE column. Let's go through each of these in turn.

F — Change word file to use. Any WordStar document file may be entered here, but the most common would be a file created during the spelling check that has the extension .ADD.

D — Change dictionary to update. SPELSTAR.DCT is the default dictionary that appears here. It takes several minutes to update and requires a large amount of disk space (about 97K).

U — Change name of new or updated dictionary. Using this option, you will end up with two dictionaries: your original, and one with the words from the original plus the words you are adding. The combined dictionary will have the name you supply here.

W — Change work drive for sort. Again, if you are working with a large dictionary, you need a large work area. With this option you can direct your sort to a drive containing a disk with ample room.

N — Create a new dictionary. You may use any name and extension for your dictionary, but if the dictionary has the extension .SUP, SpellStar will look for it on drive A, as well as on the logged drive.

A — Add words. It makes no difference if your file contains words already in the dictionary. They will be ignored, not duplicated. Of course, be sure of the spelling of the words you add.

T — Delete words. All the words contained in your word file (option **F**) will be deleted from the dictionary.

C — Combine add/delete. Words in your word file (option **F**) which are not in the dictionary will be added; words in this file that are in the dictionary will be deleted.

S — Use "S" words from "ADD" file. Only one dictionary may be updated with a single run. You indicated with the options **D** or **S** during the spelling check which words to add to a dictionary. Now you have the option of adding them to either the main or supplemental dictionary.

L — List dictionary words. As the dictionary is being updated, you have the option of listing the words on the screen. This option cannot be chosen alone. If you are merely interested in seeing the words in the dictionary, create a file with one word that is in the dictionary and go through a maintenance run to add the word.

EXERCISES

1. Run a spelling check on the file POLIT1.MM. There are no misspelled words, but there are several words for which there is no match in the dictionary. Follow the screen instructions until you are in WordStar's edit mode.

2. Delete the POLIT1.ADD file from your working disk. Run the spelling check again on POLIT1.MM. This time mark the flagged word with the **S** option. Run the dictionary maintenance option and, using POLIT1.ADD as your work file, create a supplemental dictionary and add these words to it. (*Note*: It is convenient to have the words from your letterhead, name, city, initials, and so forth, in the supplemental dictionary so that they are not flagged in every letter on which you run a spelling check.)

3. Run a spelling check on one of your own files and, if you have sufficient disk space, add the unmatched words to the main dictionary.

4. Create a file with just one correctly spelled word. Run the dictionary maintenance program and use the **A** and **L** options to list all the words in the dictionary on the screen.

5. Experiment with the various options of the spelling check and the dictionary maintenance sections of SpellStar until you are familiar with each option.

CP/M

How much you use this Appendix will depend on the version of WordStar you are using. If you are using version 1.0 or less, you will use these commands and utilities frequently. If you are using version 2.0 or greater, you will find that you can perform most of these functions directly from WordStar.

Commands

CP/M is the disk operating system you are working with. It has several built-in commands, but two are particularly important when working with WordStar.

DIR (Directory)

When the prompt symbols A> are on the screen you are in CP/M. Type **DIR**, press RETURN, and the names of all the programs that

157

are on the disk will be listed. This is useful if you have several disks containing programs and want to search through them looking for a particular program without taking the time to go into WordStar on each disk. You may also have the directory printed on the printer by typing **DIR** followed by ^**P**. When the printer has finished, type ^**P** again to return to the screen.

TYPE

This command allows you to look quickly at a file on the screen without going into WordStar. For instance, if you've forgotten what a file contains and just want to inspect it, use this command. Just type **TYPE** and the file name, and press RETURN.

If you want to stop the output as it flashes across the screen, type ^S. Press any other key to start again. If you wish to interrupt the TYPE command and look at another file, type ^C, and use the TYPE command again with the new file name.

Utilities

There are several utility programs that come with CP/M. Two that are very useful are STAT and PIP. These are separate programs and must be on your disk and loaded into the computer before they can be used. When you use the DIR command, they will appear on the directory as PIP.COM and STAT.COM.

STAT

STAT gives you the status of your disk. It details the way space on the disk has been used. Type **STAT** and press RETURN. You will now have a message on the screen telling you how much space is left on the disk in thousands of bytes. For example, the message might be

R/W SPACE:89K

The R/W tells you that you can read or write to the disk. The 89K tells you there are 89 thousand bytes of space left on the disk. One byte holds one character (letter, number, space, punctuation mark, or special symbol).

Type **STAT *.*** and press RETURN. You will get a listing of all the programs on the disk along with a statement of how much space each occupies. At the end of the listing it tells you how much space is left. The exact information you get is determined by the version of CP/M you are using. Before you type material into WordStar, be sure you use STAT to determine how much space is left on the disk. Remember, if you want to edit a 12K file and there are 10K left on the disk, WordStar will try to write the edited version to a new location and rename the old file with the BAK extension. You need space on the disk that is twice the length of your final material. Therefore, in this example there would not be enough space to edit the file.

PIP

PIP is an extremely versatile program. Here we will only consider the sections that you will find useful with WordStar. It is used primarily for copying or transferring programs between disk drives. You will find it useful for making back-up copies of your disks.

Type **PIP** and press RETURN. You will now have an asterisk (∗), the prompt for PIP, on the screen. The format of the PIP command is

A:destination disk = B:source disk

This is best explained by example. Assume you are logged into drive A (A> is displayed on the screen). Type **PIP**. You might enter any of the following commands after the asterisk:

A: = B:EXAMPLE.1

This will copy the program EXAMPLE.1 from drive B to drive A (EXAMPLE.1 is the actual filename). The program keeps the same name.

A:EXERCISE.1 = B:EXAMPLE.1

Copies the program EXAMPLE.1 from drive B to drive A and changes its name on drive A to EXERCISE.1.

B:TEST = A:EX1.WE,EX2.WE

Copies the programs EX1.WE and EX2.WE from drive A and combines them into one program on drive B called TEST.

B: = A:*.*[V]

Copies all the programs from the disk in drive A to the disk in drive B, keeping the same names for the programs. The V in brackets can be used at any time with PIP to verify that the copying was done correctly. Use this command to make back-up copies of your disks.

Index

Other Osborne/McGraw-Hill Publications

An Introduction to Microcomputers: Volume 0—The Beginner's Book
An Introduction to Microcomputers: Volume 1—Basic Concepts, 2nd Edition
An Introduction to Microcomputers: Volume 3—Some Real Support Devices
Osborne 4 & 8-Bit Microprocessor Handbook
Osborne 16-Bit Microprocessor Handbook
8089 I/O Processor Handbook
CRT Controller Handbook
68000 Microprocessor Handbook
8080A/8085 Assembly Language Programming
6800 Assembly Language Programming
Z80 Assembly Language Programming
6502 Assembly Language Programming
Z8000 Assembly Language Programming
6809 Assembly Language Programming
Running Wild—The Next Industrial Revolution
The 8086 Book
PET®/CBM™ and the IEEE 488 Bus (GPIB)
PET® Personal Computer Guide
CBM™ Professional Computer Guide
Business System Buyer's Guide
Osborne CP/M® User Guide, 2nd Edition
Apple II® User's Guide
Microprocessors for Measurement and Control
Some Common BASIC Programs
Some Common BASIC Programs—PET™/CBM™ Edition
Some Common BASIC Programs—Atari® Edition
Some Common BASIC Programs—TRS-80™ Level II Edition
Some Common BASIC Programs—Apple II Edition
Some Common BASIC Programs—IBM® Personal Computer Edition
Some Common Pascal Programs
Practical BASIC Programs
Practical BASIC Programs—TRS-80™ Level II Edition
Practical BASIC Programs—Apple II® Edition
Practical BASIC Programs—IBM® Personal Computer Edition
Practical Pascal Programs
Payroll with Cost Accounting
Accounts Payable and Accounts Receivable
General Ledger
CBASIC™ User Guide
Science and Engineering Programs—Apple II® Edition
Interfacing to S-100/IEEE 696 Microcomputers
A User Guide to the UNIX™ System
PET™ Fun and Games
Trade Secrets: How to Protect Your Ideas and Assets
Assembly Language Programming for the Apple II®
VisiCalc®: Home and Office Companion
Discover FORTH
6502 Assembly Language Subroutines
Your ATARI® Computer
The HP-IL System